AURA GARDEN GUIDES

Ray Edwards

Hanging Baskets

AURA BOOKS

Aura Garden Guides

Hanging Baskets
Ray Edwards

© 1997 Advanced Marketing (UK) Ltd.,
Bicester, England

Produced by:
Transedition Limited for
Aura Books, Bicester
and first published in 2002

Editing by:
Asgard Publishing Services, Leeds

Typesetting by:
Organ Graphic, Abingdon

10 9 8 7 6 5 4 3 2 1
Printed in Dubai

ISBN 1 901683 44 3

A beautiful basket of geraniums brings colour and life to a quiet corner of the garden.

Photographic credits
Colin Leftley: 4, 5, 7, 15, 16, 17,
18, 19, 21, 22, 23, 24, 25, 26,
27, 28, 29, 30, 31, 32, 33, 34,
35, 41, 42, 43, 44, 45, 46, 47,
48, 49, 50, 51, 52, 53, 54, 55,
56, 57, 58, 60, 63, 65 (right), 67,
68, 73, 77, 79, 84, 85, 88, 90

Peter McHoy: 2, 6, 8, 10, 11, 12,
13, 14, 36, 37, 38, 39, 40, 59,
61, 62, 64, 65 (left), 66, 69, 70,
71, 72, 74, 75, 76, 80, 81, 82,
83, 84 (top), 86, 87, 89, 91, 92,
93, 94, 95

Ray Edwards has been involved with gardening since an early age. He joined the garden staff of the Royal Botanic Gardens, Kew when he was 19, and after six and a half years he left with experience in most aspects of gardening — and with the prestigious Kew Diploma. This marked the beginning of thirty years as a professional garden writer. Before becoming a freelance gardening journalist, Ray had been technical editor of *Practical Gardening* and *Garden News*, and later became editor of *Garden Answers* and *Plants and Gardens*.

CONTENTS

High-level display

The story of hanging baskets surely begins in the distant past, with the world's most famous high-level display: the hanging gardens of Babylon — assuming, that is, that they ever existed. Authors writing long after the event say they were built by King Nebuchadnezzar for his Median wife, Amytis, to imitate the mountain landscapes of her homeland. Archaeologists think that the gardens were completed some time between 604 and 562 BC — but nothing like them was seen again until the nineteenth century.

The Victorians delighted in bold greenhouse and conservatory displays. Unusual ferns, orchids, and other tender exotics were commonly featured in hanging baskets. Strangely enough, despite their love of grand bedding schemes, they rarely used half-hardy bedders at high level, and it's only in the post-war period that this form of outdoor gardening has come to the fore.

In recent years the popularity of patios has rocketed, and this has highlighted the potential of container gardening. One of the greatest advantages of hanging baskets and other containers is their mobility. A well-stocked basket can give welcome colour in a set position for most of the season, but if you're planning an al fresco party, you can easily move them to provide a temporary display at any spot where it's safe to hang them.

Large expanses of blank wall or fencing can present a bleak outlook, yet they can often provide the support and background for an eye-stopping display of free-hanging and wall-

Natural stone makes a superb foil for this simple combination of lobelias and busy lizzies.

supported containers. Some of the finest displays I've seen have been set against old stone walls, yet wonderful effects can be achieved by using containers and planting schemes that complement modern building materials.

These days there's a vast range of plant material that is suitable for baskets. Half-hardy plants predominate, yet many hardy perennials are perfectly comfortable in their new high-rise homes, and more become available with each successive season. Almost all small or moderate-sized plants can be used for baskets, but I've restricted my list to the ones I know will succeed.

If you've never grown plants in hanging containers before, I'd advise you to make your choice from the large range of popular and easy subjects such as summer-flowering busy lizzies, or cold weather plants like winter pansies. As you become more experienced, you can gradually add one or two of the less well-known plants.

Over the years, I've been amused when people question my use of edible plants with decoratives. Why not use herbs and the occasional vegetable in your baskets? After all, many herbs provide excellent foliage displays. And you may well be amazed at the versatility of certain decoratives. The humble nasturtium proves my point: it gives a wonderful display of flower colour, and some plants even provide foliage interest,

but most amazing of all is that almost every part of the plant is edible!

Once you've been bitten by the basket bug, you'll find it hard to resist adding one or two extra subjects with the beginning of each new season. I always have a struggle not to expand the collection, and I usually lose!

A collection of wall baskets provides a colourful way to brighten up the bleak expanses created by walls and fences.

What to buy

Furnishing a hanging basket with plant material needs to be done with care. In the first place, you must be sure to choose plants that will tolerate overcrowding, but won't be so vigorous that they completely smother the display of their neighbours.

You'll find that plants with arching or pendulous growth habits are particularly suitable for hanging baskets. So are many moderately sized climbers. Plants like these can be trained to camouflage chain supports; and they can be equally effective when you encourage them to cascade over the rim and down the sides of containers.

Be a little cautious when you're choosing plants for your first hanging basket. Start with a selection of fairly inexpensive, easy-to-grow subjects such as petunias and pansies. As you start to gain experience and confidence, you can afford to be a little more adventurous, and try a few unusual fillers.

There are plenty of basket fillers to choose from, and you'll find plenty of suggestions in the later chapters of this book.

Garden centres are ideal sources of plant material for the first-time buyer, and larger centres usually stock a great variety of plants suitable for hanging baskets. The same plant will frequently be offered at different stages of growth, and this can have a considerable effect on the price. Do be careful about timing if you're buying similar plants at different stages of development. If you have a heated greenhouse or conservatory where you can grow on delicate seedlings in early spring, then you may find it practical and economical to buy small trays of seedlings at the pricking out (transplanting) stage. But if you can't provide constant warmth, there's no point in buying early!

You'll find that plants are also readily available by mail order. Most major retail seed suppliers offer seasonal bedding plants that make excellent basket

A beautiful display of pansies makes this basket stand out from the crowd.

material. As well as seedlings, plug plants in special multi-cell trays are becoming increasingly popular, along with slightly larger specimens, usually listed as 'pot ready' plants.

One advantage of buying seedlings and young plants from specialist suppliers is that each sort is despatched according to its size — and at the right time for pricking out, potting up or planting. You'll normally find that despatch dates are clearly indicated in catalogues; and so are the final order dates for individual items.

Seedlings

If you have a large number of baskets to fill, then seedlings offer an economical way to get you started — as long as you can provide the right conditions for growing on. This method is especially useful if you've had problems with seed sowing. You can also make a modest saving on greenhouse and conservatory heating costs, since established seedlings normally require slightly lower temperatures than germinating seeds.

Seedlings are usually supplied in shallow polystyrene trays. Prick them out carefully into deeper, compost-filled trays or

small pots as soon as possible after you get them.

Plug plants

Plug plants are a convenient way to buy seedlings or small plants already established in their own individual plugs of compost. The advantage of this arrangement is that you can prick them out and pot them up with the minimum disturbance to their roots — and, therefore, with almost no check to their growth.

Up to four sizes of plug plants are available, depending on the supplier. The first size (sometimes called mini-plugs) will usually contain 100 or so established seedlings, which eliminates any need to sow and prick out the plants. The next size will give you fewer than 50 seedlings, but they'll be well developed and ready for transplanting into trays or pots. The third size provides 20 or so strong, young plants large

enough to be planted directly into hanging containers.

The largest mail-order plants arrive well rooted in substantial compost plugs or special Jiffy pots. Depending on their size, they will usually arrive in packs of five or ten plants. These so-called 'pot ready' plants are particularly suitable for direct planting into baskets.

Established plants

You'll need to grow on half-hardly seedlings and plug plants under cover until frost-free conditions prevail outside. If you can't offer them the protection of a greenhouse, conservatory or porch, don't buy seasonal summer bedders until late spring or early summer.

Half-hardy annual plants like petunias and lobelias are widely available as established flowering specimens in trays or pots. Modern trays usually consist of several strips, each holding a

Right: Plug plants are supplied in handy plastic trays, and ready planted in their own plugs of compost.

number of individual plants.

Strip trays are particularly useful if you only need a few individuals of each plant, since it's easy to detach each strip from the parent tray. However, if you want plants of a particular colour or shade, then you may find that individual potted specimens are the best buy.

Pots are also an advantage where you need fairly advanced plants to give an almost immediate effect; again, the roots will receive little or no check at planting time. You can now buy established plants in packs of flimsy plastic square pots that are joined together for easy transportation. However, larger specimens still tend to be offered in individual terracotta or rigid plastic containers.

Buying tips

When you're choosing plants from garden centres, stores and market stalls, the following tips will help you to find the ones that will establish themselves quickly and reward you with a long display period.

Don't be tempted to buy seedlings, plug plants or pot-ready specimens too early. Most half-hardy summer basket plants prefer a minimum growing temperature of at least 50°F (9°C). If you can't give it to them, it's better to wait until the weather warms up. If you don't, you could incur heavy losses.

Right: A splash of colour from these pansies enlivens an otherwise featureless wall.

8

Refuse any plants that show signs of discoloration or blemishing on stems or foliage. Watch for signs of pests (particularly aphids) and diseases.

Drooping stems and leaves suggest plants have not been looked after, and that watering has been erratic. Too much water is as bad as too little; these plants will have poor, or even non-existent, root systems.

If, on the other hand, you find that the roots have penetrated the base of the container to form a tangled mat, the plant will invariably be damaged when you remove it. This isn't usually fatal, but it will result in a check to growth, and the plant will take longer to get re-established.

Ideally, try to buy plants with sturdy stems, well clothed with leaves to the base. Depending on their normal growth habit, young plants should be fairly bushy and uniform in size. Undue lankiness, or weak, straggly growth usually indicates poor growing conditions.

Established pot-grown specimens of plants such as *Pelargonium* (geranium) and *Petunia* are usually sold in flower. So are vigorous half-hardy summer bedders such as *Impatiens* (Busy lizzie) and the fibrous-rooted *Begonia semperflorens*. For preference, choose strip and tray plants that show a few open blooms, but plenty of buds.

Seedlings and plug plants should never show signs of buds, and pot-ready specimens should show no more than the first signs of buds.

Mail order hints

Ask for catalogues as early as possible. It's a good idea to order early as well, especially if you want new or novelty basket plants that are likely to sell out quickly.

Take note of the last order date of each item, and keep to it strictly to avoid disappointment.

If you don't have strong preferences regarding plant combinations, use one of the special basket collections offered by most seedling and plant suppliers.

Unpack mail-order plant consignments as soon as you receive them. Check that you have what you ordered, and that it's in good condition. If you're not happy with the plants, send them back with a covering letter immediately. Before transplanting or planting, keep seedlings and plants in a partially shaded spot for a day or two. This will allow them to readjust to full light conditions.

Starting from scratch

If you have the facilities to raise your own basket plants by means of seeds and cuttings, you may find it very rewarding to do so. If you need large numbers of plants, it'll also help to reduce the overall cost quite a lot.

Temperature tips

If you don't have a heated greenhouse, you can raise a moderate number of plants in the home, but it's important to keep temperatures fairly constant. Severe fluctuations in temperature will inhibit seed germination rather than encouraging it, and even when it's successful the resultant seedlings may not grow very well.

Early in the year, it can be expensive to keep a greenhouse or conservatory at the high temperatures that you'll need for propagation. You can save money by restricting the heat to a relatively small area. In practice this means buying an electrically heated propagator (or, perhaps, building your own).

There's a wide choice of proprietary propagators, and several are specially designed to fit indoor window-sills. For the best results, look for models with a thermostatically controlled warming cable fitted in the base.

Ideally you should be able to provide a temperature range between 65-75°F (18-24°C) to raise a wide selection of plants from seeds and cuttings. However, many of the easier half-hardy subjects, and most hardy plants, have more modest heat requirements.

Containers

Always start with sound, clean containers. Plastic pots and trays are inexpensive, but rigid plastic offers the best value: you can continue to use it for several years. It's best to discard the flimsy type as soon as you've finished with them.

Terracotta pots tend to be expensive. They're also more difficult to keep clean than plastic types, and good hygiene is essential for successful propagation. Store them under cover to avoid frost damage.

Nowadays, wooden trays are rarely used, but if you do want to use them for seed sowing and pricking out they must be sound, clean and treated with a timber preservative that is non-toxic to plants. Untreated timber trays are likely to carry harmful disease organisms; and they'll eventually rot and fall to pieces — usually at the most inopportune times!

Plastic or polystyrene trays are preferable for seed sowing and rooting cuttings, and these come in a range of sizes. Half trays are ideal for small numbers of seedlings and cuttings. Alternatively you may prefer to use one of the modern multi-cell trays for sowing individual large seeds or solitary cuttings.

Left: *sowing seeds in a plastic tray.*

Compost

Peat-based composts are ideal for raising both seeds and cuttings, but if you're looking for alternatives then coir (coconut fibre) and traditional loam-based John Innes composts are very satisfactory. I generally recommend the multi-purpose or seed and cutting composts. Any compost that you use must be well-drained, and contain a balanced amount of fertiliser to give seedlings and cuttings a good start.

You may find that some difficult cuttings can benefit from home-mixed composts, particularly if they are inclined to rot off at the base before rooting occurs. I find that equal parts of moss peat and sharp sand, perlite or vermiculite in a well-drained mix can be very useful.

Compressed peat compost 'pots' such as the Jiffy 7 type offer a handy combination of pot and compost. They're supplied in the form of dry, compressed disks enveloped in a fine plastic mesh. When you moisten them they swell up to about four times their dry volume.

Jiffy 7 pots are very useful for striking cuttings of geraniums

Preparing modules in a multi-cell tray for sowing.

and similar half-hardy shrubby subjects, and for sowing individual large seeds. They're also ideal for growing on the pricked out (transplanted) seedlings of most bedding plants — and of course, you can plant them directly into baskets.

11

Success with seeds

Always start with high-quality seeds from a reputable supplier. When you're buying seeds in a shop or garden centre, check the packeting date on the outer packet. Don't open the packet until sowing time, and store any remaining seed in a dry, cool and frost free place.

Fl hybrid varieties will give the most uniform plants in terms of colour, habit and size. Self-saved seeds collected from Fl hybrid plants will not give identical offspring, so it's always best to start afresh with a new batch of seeds each year. However, perennial Fl varieties of pelargonium and fuchsia can sometimes be propagated by means of cuttings.

Fill your container almost to the top with moist (not wet) compost, and gently firm it level to within about 1/2 in (13 mm) of the rim. If the compost looks a little dry at this point, water it gently with a fine rose (sprinkler head) on your watering can. Let the excess water drain away before you sow the seeds.

You can sow larger seeds into individual containers, or space them out in trays. Smaller seeds should be scattered very thinly over the surface. Dust-like seeds (begonia seeds, for instance) can be very difficult to sow evenly, but if you mix them with a little dry, fine silver sand the job becomes much easier. Alternatively look for specially pelleted seeds: they're a lot easier to handle.

You shouldn't cover fine seeds with compost, but others will need a light sprinkling. Apply it through a garden sieve. When you've covered them with an even depth of compost (about twice the diameter of the seeds), firm it very gently with a piece of board or plastic.

As most seeds need dark conditions to germinate successfully, cover the containers with brown paper or coloured plastic sheeting. Common basket plants that need light for germination include *Impatiens* (Busy lizzie), *Mimulus* (musk or monkey flower) and begonias.

Depending on seed type and season, put your containers in a propagator or a frame. If you're standing them on an open staging bench or a shelf in your greenhouse, cover them with a sheet of rigid plastic or glass. This will stop the compost drying out too quickly.

Maintain the temperatures that are recommended on the seed packet. Once germination takes place, remove any paper, or your seedlings will be pale and weak when they grow. Clear condensation from plastic or glass covers regularly. This stops any drips falling on the seedlings, and so prevents problems with rot. Once the seedlings are growing away, remove any plastic or glass covering completely.

Water with a fine rose sprinkler on the watering can, or a hand mister spray for very small and delicate seedlings. Prick out seedlings as soon as

Busy lizzie (Impatiens)

possible (usually at the first true leaf stage). Handle them very carefully, holding the leaves rather than the stems.

Grow on seedlings at the recommended germination temperature for about a week, then move them into slightly cooler conditions as they become established in their new containers.

Cuttings clues

Cuttings are an easy way to increase the numbers of many perennial basket plants — and often the only way to raise named varieties that aren't available as seeds.

In addition to pelargoniums, other half-hardy perennials that you may like to try include

certain forms of petunia, double-flowered lobelia, and a selection of hardy basket fillers such as trailing types of *Campanula*, *Viola* (pansies and violas) and *Hedera* (ivy).

Timing will depend on the type of plant you're dealing with, but cuttings are usually taken in spring and summer. In spring you'll need artificial heat to root half-hardy and tender plants, but cuttings taken in late spring and summer will usually be quite happy in a cold frame or an unheated greenhouse.

You must only take cuttings from healthy plants. Never use any material if the plant shows the slightest sign of weakness or disfigurement, particularly if

Taking geranium (pelargonium) cuttings.

it is known to be vulnerable to certain fungal or viral diseases.

In general, shoot-tip cuttings are used for basket plants. These can range in length from 1 to 6 in (2.5 to 15 cm) depending on the material that you're preparing. Ideally you should choose shoots without buds or blooms, since these will make the best cuttings. If you don't have enough unflowered material, use the best

13

shoots, and trim off buds or flowers carefully.

Use a clean, sharp blade to prepare cuttings. Trim off the lower part of each stem to a point just below a convenient leaf joint. A straight cut is usually best. If your cutting is very leafy, you can remove the lower foliage just before you put it into the compost.

Tender green shoots provide what are known as 'soft' cuttings. However, many shrubby basket plants can also be increased by means of partially ripened shoots in summer. In these shoots the lower part is firm and slightly woody. This type of cutting often roots more rapidly if the wound is dipped into a hormone rooting powder or gel.

Prepare pots or trays of suitable size and depth with compost, and make planting holes with a small dibber or pencil. You'll find that a layer of silver sand on the surface of the compost is often beneficial; it will trickle down to the base of each planting hole, and help to minimise rotting at the base of the cuttings.

Violas on display in an attractive half basket.

Push in the cuttings so that the lowest leaf is just above the surface of the compost. Gently firm in at the base using a pencil or dibber.

After you've watered in the cuttings with a fine-rosed can, put the containers in a frame or a propagator to root. If you don't have a covered propagator, seal the containers in a clean, clear plastic bag which is supported on a framework of four split canes. When the cuttings show signs of active growth, this is usually the sign that rooting is under way.

Once your cuttings have formed a decent root system, transplant them into small individual pots or multi-cell trays. They'll grow on into vigorous young plants suitable for direct planting into baskets.

This basket shows a simple, but effective use of massed blue lobelias punctuated by double soft pink fuchsias.

Harden plants off

It's essential for all young plants raised under cover to undergo a period of temperature adjustment before you put them outside. This is called the 'hardening-off period', and it's particularly important for all tender basket plants started off in late winter or early spring. Half-hardy plants raised in spring should be gradually acclimatised to outdoor conditions. Do this by moving them into a cold frame as the danger of frost recedes in late spring. Alternatively you can stand containers in a sheltered part of the garden in the daytime, but move them back under glass at night until all danger of frost has passed.

Choosing containers

Hanging baskets are made in a very wide range of designs and materials. Your choice will be partly determined by the amount you're willing to pay, but there are other, important factors you ought to consider. What are the floral effects you want to achieve? And is a particular type of container suitable for the site where you want to put it?

Besides free-hanging baskets suspended from brackets, there are a number of static types that meet a few particular needs. For instance, you'll find fixed baskets more practical on a windy site, and half baskets provide an ideal planting area to brighten up large, uninteresting expanses of wall or fencing.

Although the emphasis is on baskets, other kinds of hanging container are widely available. These may prove more satisfactory indoors, or on very exposed sites where open mesh baskets tend to dry out too rapidly.

Containers come in many sizes, too: the diameter of popular open mesh basket models ranges from about 10 to 20 in (25 to 50 cm). However, larger designs are not uncommon, and the ornate wrought-iron hayracks are often much larger than traditional baskets.

*Open-mesh, plastic-covered wire models (**below, left**) are the most popular types of hanging basket. Those with flat bases provide a stable platform when you're planting up. Real or simulated hayrack baskets (**below, right**) are ideal for creating a rustic effect. They're also offered as cauldron baskets.*

Metalwork

Traditional wire baskets are either galvanised or plastic-coated to prolong their working life. From time to time collapsible, fine-mesh models appear on the market, but you're more likely to be offered rigid, open-mesh designs in your local garden centre or store.

You can buy wire baskets with curved or flat bases. A flat base gives you a stable platform when you're planting; it's also easier to stand on a greenhouse bench, when your baskets are getting established before you put them in their final positions.

Bird-cage ornamental planters are an attractive variant on wire hanging baskets. Although they're a little more expensive, they look very effective both indoors and outdoors. They're usually made from a wider gauge wire coated in white, black or green plastic.

Other variants include deep hanging cauldrons made from heavy-duty steel wire, and a number of static, pedestal-mounted wire baskets and cauldrons. These are very decorative, and you'll find them particularly effective on patios.

Real and simulated hayracks are also excellent for mounting on walls to create a rustic effect, and you'll find various ornate styles on offer in wrought iron. Larger models can hold a substantial amount of compost, which makes them ideal for large-scale plantings.

Plastic

This material is widely used in the manufacture of hanging containers. Styles range from designs that emulate traditional wire mesh baskets to solid wall-mounted types. The basket models will need a liner, but solid models are self-contained, and may include such useful features as integral self-watering facilities and drip trays.

Many attractive, inexpensive containers like this fold-away plastic leaf style are available for house-plants.

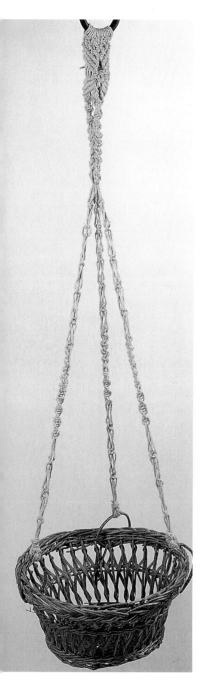

Solid plastic hanging containers with drip-tray attachments are particularly useful for displaying trailing conservatory subjects and houseplants. For one thing they reduce the risk of damage to furniture and floor coverings. Many styles are available: models with moulded pockets or cups in the side walls will give you extra planting positions.

Plastic hanging pots and troughs are widely available in a range of colours — including white, green, black, brown and terracotta — and differently textured surface finishes.

Two fairly recent innovations have become very popular for patio displays: hanging flower towers and flower pouches. These are made from flexible plastic sheeting. They're ideal as free-hanging features in a sheltered position, or for securing against a wall or fence.

A typical cylindrical pouch holds about 2 gallons (8 litres)

*Wickerwork hanging containers (**left**) are ideal for displaying conservatory and indoor plants.*

*(**Opposite page**) The white wall makes a stark contrast to this colourful container, a timber wall basket amply clothed with hardy trailing creeping Jenny and a selection of half-hardy summer bedders.*

of compost, and provides ten pre-cut planting positions.

Terracotta

This traditional material is frequently employed to make ornamental hanging bowls and pots, not to mention a very attractive range of wall containers. You'll find several variants on offer, but be careful. Some have no provision for basal drainage, and these will need very careful watering. Those with planting holes in the sides are very useful if you want overall plant cover.

Terracotta hanging containers are often supported by macramé slings, which adds to the general decorative effect when they're used indoors.

Timber

Slat baskets have been used to hold greenhouse and conservatory plants for several centuries,. They're ideal for epiphytic plants, because in the wild these plants grow perched on the branches of trees. Plants that need this very sharp drainage include many types of bromeliad (urn plants and their relatives), epiphytic orchids, and tree-dwelling ferns such as *Nephrolepis*.

However, a number of very attractive timber baskets have been designed for outdoor use. Most of these are wall-mounted — but any timber basket should be regularly checked for signs of rot. It's also a very good idea to apply a non-toxic timber preservative every year.

Choosing liners

All open mesh and timber-slatted containers need a liner to stop compost falling out. Liners also help to stop undue loss of moisture from the compost, as well as making it easier to plant up your baskets.

In the past, moss was a cheap, natural lining for hanging baskets. These days it can only be collected and sold under licence. As a result, several alternative proprietary materials have appeared on the market. Many are biodegradable, which makes them more acceptable to conservation-minded gardeners.

Some liners are made to look like moss, and can be treated in a similar way. Products made from less flexible materials can be pre-cut to shape, allowing them to fit snugly and neatly into your containers.

Moss

Despite the conservation issue, various moss species are still collected, and they're undoubtedly the most attractive lining material available. However, I find that moss must be applied generously to do its job properly, and prevent loss of compost from open-mesh wire baskets.

With a moss liner it's easy to plant through the sides of the basket, but you must keep the liner moist to keep it looking good — and working effectively. Sphagnum moss species are the best for retaining moisture, but

they're not as easy to find as they used to be.

Wool

Several types of proprietary liner are made from biodegradable wool materials. Some have quite an open texture; it's easy to plant through them, but I normally add an inner liner of plastic film. This gives additional strength, and encourages better water retention when the plants are in full growth.

Products of this kind are often described as 'wool moss', and they can be handled in much the same way as natural moss.

Others, manufactured from stiff felted wool fabric, aren't as nice to look at but tend to do a better job of retaining your compost. The stiff wool products are pre-cut in the familiar 'petal' fashion to make installation easy. Wool products are available in natural greenish shades or in black.

Wood fibre

These rigid moulded liners are tidy and convenient for wire baskets, though sometimes they don't look very natural. The position of each hole is clearly marked, and partly cut through to make planting easier, but in some cases I've found that they don't always line up with the gaps between the wires.

This type of liner holds compost well. It's best to use plug

plants with them: more mature specimens tend to be too large to slip easily through the holes.

Coir fibre

Natural coir fibre liners are a fairly recent innovation, and there are several types available. One design comes as a brown, pre-cut circular inlay. Alternatives include coco moss, made from loose coir and dyed green.

Coir products are attractive and natural-looking, but you'll need to cut planting holes for your plants. Use them with an inner liner of plastic film: this helps keep your compost moist during late spring and summer.

Foam

Foam liners come pre-cut to suit both conventional baskets and half-baskets (for walls). This material absorbs moisture readily, but allows it to evaporate quite rapidly in warm conditions. As the material stretches, it's easy enough to break holes with my fingers and push the plants through.

Compost retention is good if you install the liner with a good 'petal' overlap . Foam liners are usually green, but I don't find them very attractive until the plants become established. One way to give them more character in the early stages is to use them as an inner liner for a thin layer of natural moss.

Composition liners

This material is widely used in the manufacture of horticultural growing rings and disposable plant pots. Composition liners are readily available from most garden centres and stores. They come pre-cut, and with a generous number of clearly marked planting positions.

This group of semi-rigid liners come in sizes ranging from 10 in (25 cm) to 20 in (50 cm) in diameter, and there are several more designed to fit different sizes of half-basket (for walls). I find these inexpensive liners

A selection of basket liners: (clockwise from top left) foam, fibre, coco fibre, coloured coco fibre, and wool moss. The disk underneath, at lower left, is a pre-formed coco fibre lining.

ideal for seasonal plant collections. They're highly biodegradable, which is probably a good thing — but it does mean that they rarely give more than a single season's service.

Plastic

Several companies make moulded rigid plastic liners that fit neatly into wire or plastic mesh baskets. If you treat this type of liner with care, it will give years of faithful service. Unfortunately there is rarely any provision for side planting, so this design is not ideal if you're looking to create a large display.

You may find it rather difficult to line baskets that have very wide spacing between the wires, and some of the larger hayrack designs. In my experience it's best to deal with these

either by installing plastic sheeting, or by using sheets of fine woven netting specially made for greenhouse shading.

This netting comes in various mesh sizes and you can easily mould it to the shape of any container. It's also easy to make holes in it, and when I'm planting up birdcage basket designs I routinely use it as an inner liner in combination with natural moss.

Plain plastic sheeting is cheap, and you can use it to line almost any basket, but until your plants grow big enough to hide it, it can look rather unattractive. Black is the most unobtrusive colour, but if you've chosen very fast-growing plants that will hide the sides, you could choose green or white instead.

Compost clues

You can't expect superb results if you start with anything less than a top quality compost. No amount of feeding will make up for starting plants off in old, spent compost left over from the previous season or, worse still, if you try to cut costs by using soil collected from your garden!

It's important to think about weight when you're planting up a hanging basket. Lightweight, loam-free composts are generally the most popular for short-term seasonal displays, but I haven't found them so reliable for sustaining perennials over a period of several years.

A number of proprietary compost mixes have been formulated specifically for hanging baskets and other containers. These are ideal for the less experienced gardener, but as long as you water and feed regularly throughout the growing season, any decent multi-purpose compost should prove equally successful.

Peat composts are lightweight, but tend to dry out rather quickly in warm and windy conditions, and when they're crowded with vigorous plants. You may be offered pure moss peat, or blended products that combine moss and sedge peat.

Other combinations that may suit your purpose are peat-based composts with added silver sand, perlite or vermiculite to improve drainage. All of them should contain a balanced complement of nutrients to ensure healthy growth and flowering. However, if you want to grow a number of ericaceous

*Multi-purpose composts (**below, left**) are widely available from garden centres and stores. These are ideal for seeds, cuttings and mature plants.*

*Special basket composts (**below, right**) with added water-retentive granules will allow you to water less often in hot weather.*

plants, such as heaths and heather, look for one of the specially formulated proprietary lime-free composts.

Coir fibre offers a peat- and loam-free alternative. It's also very light, and tends to dry out rather more slowly than peat. Again, a balanced fertiliser is essential for success.

Loam-based composts based on the famous John Innes formulae are a little heavy for general use in baskets, but make an exception if you want a collection of long-lived shrubby or herbaceous perennials. Be sure to compensate for the extra weight of soil by using stronger chain supports and brackets.

To my mind, it's better to solve the problem of long-term plantings by using a modern compost mix that contains a high proportion of peat or coir fibre, and some loam to give extra 'body'. These composts are also excellent for sustaining large numbers of plants over a single season, though here, again, regular feeding and watering are essential.

Buying hints

- Never use soil from your garden to make up your own compost for hanging baskets.
- Don't be tempted to use old, spent compost, or the remains of growing bags.
- Always buy new batches of compost that have been stored under cover: faded bags are a sure sign of old stock. Refuse bags that have been standing outdoors for any length of time, particularly those that are saturated.
- For preference buy compost mixes that include trace elements as well as major plant nutrients.
- If the mix includes a wetting agent, the compost will be easier to re-moisten if it dries out.
- If the mix includes a moisture-retaining product you won't need to water quite so often.

If you prefer not to use peat or loam-based compost, look out for coir types like the special Wessex basket formulation.

Step-by-step planting

What you plant is very much a matter of personal choice. My rule is to be as generous as you can afford to be when you're stocking your baskets. The vigour and eventual size of the plants you choose will partly determine how many you can include, but the size of your container is just as important.

As a guide, I normally reckon on up to eighteen summer plants to furnish a 14 in (35 cm) wide open-mesh basket. You'll want far fewer if the walls (or the liner) are solid. For indoor hanging pots and baskets it's usually best to restrict yourself

Planting — ten steps to success

1 Stand flat-bottomed wire baskets on a firm and level surface, or support them with a large flower pot, a bucket or a special wire frame as illustrated. Spread out a wad of moss to give good coverage, or insert a proprietary liner.

3 Add water-retaining granules and slow or controlled-release fertiliser when using peat-based compost for summer displays. To plant a 14 in (35 cm) wide basket you'll need enough compost to almost fill a 3 gallon (13.5 litre) bucket.

5 If you've lined the container with live moss, it helps to use your fingers to lift and firm the compost in towards the basket sides. This will ensure that the sides remain strong. Don't push the compost down hard: it will over-compact the mixture.

2 If you're using live moss, cut out a circle of plastic sheeting and position it to create a trough about 1 in (2.5 cm) deep. This will act rather like a reservoir, and help to stop the compost drying out in summer.

4 Mix all the ingredients thoroughly before filling the basket with compost. Mound up the compost slightly at the centre. It's a good idea to keep any excess so you can use it for topping up later on.

6 Tidy the rim by teasing moss up the inside walls until it's about 1 in (2.5 cm) proud of the top wire. This gives a soft cushion for plant stems spilling over the rim. Repeat stage five to re-firm the compost.

to a single plant. However, what appears to be a single house-plant will often, on careful inspection, turn out to be several closely planted cuttings.

A careful mix of different flowering and foliage plants will create stunning displays out-doors, but in certain locations, or on special occasions, solo plantings may prove more effective. You could for exam-ple, use impatiens or violas in a single colour. A slightly more adventurous approach might be to use varieties of slightly different shades to give a gradu-ated range of colour, say from pure white through to pink and purple.

One rather unusual display method involves wiring two planted baskets firmly together. This creates what could be described as a 'globe of colour'. The method is particularly effective for solo plantings, but do take care to ensure that the compost is kept uniformly moist.

Contrasting flower colours and foliage textures always look effective, but you can achieve equally stunning effects by using complementary colours and textures, such as silver-felted helichrysums and pale-pink-flowered petunias.

Colour co-ordinated plantings have proved very popular in recent years, and you can get very attractive results by care-fully selecting containers and supports in colours that com-plement the plants.

Planting ideas

I have made the following suggestions for seasonal plant-ing using plants that you should find are widely available from garden centres and mail-order suppliers.

Summer selection 1

Fuchsia 'Pink Marshmallow'; pelargonium 'L'Elegante'; *Lysimachia* 'Outback Sunset'; *Bacopa* 'Snowflake'; petunia 'Purple Wave'; verbena 'Siss-inghurst Pink'; *Convolvulus sabatius*; nasturtium *Tropae-olum majus* 'Alaska'; *Glechoma hederacea* 'Variegata'; and double-flowered *Impatiens* (Busy lizzie) 'Rosette'.

7   Plant from the bottom of baskets to the top. If a plant has a very large root system you have to tease away some of the com-post to insert the plant through the side of the basket.

9   Gradually work up the sides of the basket, and finish off with the top plants. Use your fingers to scoop out planting holes for top plants, and never try to force the root balls down into the compost.

8   Make the holes through your liner as large as possible. Plant the bottom layer just above the plastic sheet reservoir. Don't push any plant too far into the compost, or the base of the stem may begin to rot.

10   Plant spring bulbs 2 to 3 in (5 to 7.5 cm) deep; make holes with fingers or a dibber. If you plant two different kinds, plant larger bulbs deeper. Water basket thoroughly before hanging it in place.

(**Above**) *A well-furnished basket of colour co-ordinated petunias and verbenas*

(**Below**) *Winter/spring collection 2*

Summer selection 2

Top: fuchsia 'Golden Marinka'; pink and white pelargonium 'Balcon' or 'Mini Cascade'; zonal pelargonium 'Venus' or 'Maverick Star'; tuberous begonia 'Sensation'; *Diascia* 'Lilac Mist', and *Impatiens* (Busy lizzie) 'Mosaic Lilac'. Sides: lobelia 'White Fountain' and/or blue 'Sapphire'; *Bacopa* 'Snowflake'; verbena 'Tapien' or 'Imagination'; *Calceolaria* 'Midas' or 'Sunshine'; and *Helichrysum petiolare*.

Winter/spring collection 1

Osmanthus heterophylla 'Goshiki'; *Hedera* 'Ceridwen'; mixed 'Universal' pansies; *Bellis perennis* 'Pomponette White' and/or 'Pomponette Rose'; *Ajuga pyramidalis* 'Burgundy', plus a selection of dwarf bulbs such as crocus, narcissi or early tulips.

Winter/spring collection 2

This selection is illustrated on the left
Top: (E) *Euonymus fortunei* 'Emerald 'n' Gold'; (G) *Helichrysum italicum serotinum* (curry plant); (F) *Hebe* 'Green Globe'; (D) *Salvia officinalis* 'Tricolor'; (H) red 'Ultima' pansies, and ten muscari bulbs. Sides: (B) *Lamium maculatum* 'White Nancy'; (A) *Ajuga reptans* 'Multicolor' ('Rainbow'); and (C) blue 'Ultima' pansies.

Secure supports

Safety should be foremost in your mind when you're arranging supports for your hanging baskets. It's essential to make sure that they are securely hung, particularly if you're using the larger sizes, which will hold relatively high volumes of compost.

There are many different ways to support hanging baskets. Your choice will depend on the position (e.g. on a wall, a fence, or a beam), the site, and the proposed height of your display.

Whatever method you choose, remember that the strength of the support should be dictated by the estimated maximum weight of your container.

Obviously, then, it's useful to have a rough idea of how much the hanging basket will weigh when the compost is moist, and supporting a full complement of mature plants. Luckily this isn't as hard as it sounds! Simply put a moist, compost-laden basket on your kitchen scales at planting time, then reckon on half or

as much again in plant weight.

If this doesn't help you to decide on the strength of your supports, you can seek the advice of your local builders' merchants. They're usually pleased to help.

Brackets

Metal brackets are very popular way to support hanging containers of all types, but remember that you need to choose them according to the size of baskets. Brackets come in a variety of styles and colours, and they're widely available in packs, complete with all the necessary screws and wall plugs.

2   Drill hole with masonry bit

1   Mark position on wall or fence

4   Fix bracket with screws

3   Insert wall plug

5   Hang basket in position

6   Fitting 'hi-lo' suspension unit

Mixed baskets of petunia ('Surfinia') give a warm welcome at the front door.

Top-mounted baskets offer a novel variant on the bracket. Here the container is firmly secured to the top of the bracket, providing a stable growing platform. This can be much safer than free-hanging baskets on exposed and windy sites.

When you're securing brackets to a wall, drill out the holes and push in wall plugs that are suitable for the screw sizes you're using. As a guide, brackets installed to support a small basket will need screws at least $2^{1}/_{2}$ in (6.5 cm) long. Brass screws are best. If you use anything else, check every year for signs of deterioration.

Brackets should also be checked every year; if you find any sign of rust, remove it with a wire brush. Once you've cleaned off any rust, and any flaking paint, apply a rust prevention treatment and one or two coats of gloss paint.

As well as wrought iron, cast aluminium, and other types of metal bracket, you'll also find timber and cane designs. These are intended to give decorative support to lightweight baskets and hanging pots indoors. If you use timber brackets to create a rustic effect outside, make sure they are periodically treated with a rot-resistant preservative, or paint them to maintain their attractive appearance and prevent deterioration.

Hooks

If you're going to hang baskets under the eaves of your house, from overhead timber beams, or from a ceiling indoors, specially designed hooks are usually safer than ordinary domestic designs.

Swivel hooks, for example, come in ornate designs that look very attractive either indoors or outside. If you can live with a less aesthetic effect, you can use one of the inexpensive plastic-covered designs widely available from DIY stores. These heavy-duty, general-purpose designs are normally used in garages and workshops.

For heavy baskets needing sturdy support, use substantial galvanised ring screws or bolts. If the screws don't have a plastic or galvanised coating, use durable brass or alloy designs.

Wall-hanging containers like half-baskets and wall tubs also need secure fixings. Most are fixed firmly into position using screws and wall plugs, but it's safe to hang smaller baskets on stout brass screw-hooks.

28

Pedestals and stands

Although we usually associate hanging baskets with high-level display, there's no reason not to use them below head height.

In this context basket pedestals and stands can provide useful, mobile supports which you can move around your garden and patio to create instant hanging colour at a moment's notice.

Two main types are available. The first provides one or more built-in brackets from which you can suspend your hanging baskets. The other offers a selection of designs featuring fixed or removable, ring-supported containers. There are even 'hybrid' versions featuring a large fixed basket at ground level and a central stand bearing one or more support brackets for free-hanging baskets.

Suspension

Closed-link chains are the ideal way to support open-mesh hanging baskets, especially when they're used for large, heavy containers. Metal chains should be made of brass, or galvanised, to ensure long service. Give all chains an annual overhaul, and check them for signs of deterioration.

Some basket designs feature a single central suspension wire hook. This type is usually painted, or surface coated, in the same colour as the container. This makes it less conspicuous, but you must take great care not to overload it with heavy compost mixes and crowded plantings.

Chain and single-hook support systems can both be used to suspend one basket under another. If you've got enough headroom, a multiple or tiered basket display can be very effective, but do be sure to give careful consideration to the strength of any supporting structures and the methods you use to hang the baskets.

Solid-walled plastic containers usually feature solid plastic strap hangers in place of chains. These moulded designs clip or slot into grooves and holes set in the container rim, but they are only really practical where the volume of compost used and plantings are fairly restricted. Even the best grades of plastic will gradually degrade over a number of seasons, so check them every year and replace them as necessary.

Macramé support nets and straps are very attractive, but they're really only suitable for your conservatory or for displays inside the house. They're widely available from the larger garden centres and florist's shops, and come in a fantastic range of materials and designs.

Spring-loaded suspension systems

You can easily obtain proprietary spring-loaded suspension systems that allow baskets to be lowered to a convenient height for watering and other maintenance work. Once you've finished the job, you just raise the basket gently back to its original position.

A spring-loaded suspension system makes watering a very simple and convenient task.

This type of aid is very useful if you find it difficult to climb up steps or onto stools, but please do remember that weight will once again impose restrictions on their use. Always read the manufacturer's directions carefully, and follow the recommended weight limitations exactly.

Remember to weigh the basket when the compost is completely saturated; and remember that you must allow for a gradual increase in weight as the plants continue to grow.

29

Feeding facts

As most proprietary composts only contain sufficient nutrients to maintain healthy growth and flowering for a limited period, it is important that you make up any shortfalls by supplementary feeding. Strength of feed and frequency of application will depend on several factors, the major ones being the frequency of watering, temperature, and rate of plant growth.

As a rough guide, vigorous basket plants grown under cover will benefit from regular feeding during the spring and summer months, with occasional applications in autumn and winter. Outdoors the conditions will be markedly different in summer and winter, so feeding must be adjusted accordingly.

During the warm summer months, rapid plant growth and almost continuous flowering will soon deplete reserves of nutrients in the compost. Frequent watering will exacerbate the problem further through the action of leaching, so it's very important to make up losses by regularly feeding with a suitable fertiliser.

As the weather cools in autumn and turns cold in winter, reduced plant growth and an infrequent need for watering will result in minimal nutrient loss. Consequently you will not need to begin supplementary feeding overwintered hardy display plants until conditions warm up in spring.

A general balanced fertiliser is safe to use on most plants, and if the product contains a complement of minor and trace elements, so much the better.

High nitrogen fertilisers will encourage plant growth, while those with a high potash content (tomato feeds) will encourage better flower colour and (in the case of vegetables and fruit) fruit production.

In recent years a range of fertiliser products have been produced that take the guesswork out of feeding plants in hanging baskets and other types of container. These are specially formulated to encourage vigorous growth and prolific flowering in densely planted containers, but similar results are perfectly possible using the fertilisers listed below.

*Liquid fertiliser formulations (**below, left and centre**) are quickly taken up by growing plants, but ensure compost is moist before application. Controlled release fertiliser granules such as Osmocote Plus (**below, right**) provide nutrients over a long period.*

Types of fertiliser

Liquid feeding is the most popular method of providing a constant supply of nutrients, but it's important that dry compost is thoroughly moistened before you apply liquid formulations. Failure to re-wet dry compost will result in much of the valuable feed running away and being wasted.

Various products are available, including concentrated liquid types that just need diluting in water, and water-soluble dry products. Read bottle or packet instructions carefully about dilution rates and dosages, and never be tempted to exceed the amount stated.

Some liquid fertilisers can also be used as a quick-acting foliar feed, but again check the dilution rates very carefully or leaf scorch may occur. And for the same reason, take care not to apply foliar sprays when plants are exposed to bright sun.

Dry fertiliser formulations may also be used, but these will need a little extra time to break down into a form that can be readily absorbed by the plants. Apply to the surface of the compost and work in using a sharp tool or plant label. Fertiliser pellets and tablets are a variation on dry formulations, but make sure that you push them into the compost at evenly spaced intervals to achieve uniform distribution of nutrients.

Modern slow-release fertiliser granules that supply nutrients to

Adding moisture-retentive products like these will benefit densely planted baskets, especially during warm weather.

plants over a period of several months are very useful if you tend to forget the need to feed! This type contain a balanced mixture of the major nutrients necessary for growth and flowering, plus important trace elements to help maintain health, and have the added advantage of only releasing those nutrients when temperatures are high enough to initiate growth.

I have found slow-release products are best mixed in with the compost at planting time, then as growth appears to slow, a further application can be gently worked into the surface of the compost.

Ways to water

The single most important factor in getting the best out of your hanging baskets is probably correct watering. In summer, when plant growth is most rampant, the combination of warm weather and crowded, thirsty root systems will rapidly dry out your compost, so a daily inspection is essential.

At the height of summer you'll probably need to water some baskets once, or even twice, daily, especially if they're supporting a large number of plants. You can help your plants to fight back against drought by using compost that contains water-retaining granules or gel.

You must also be able to re-wet compost that has accidentally been allowed to dry out completely; this problem usually arises with peat-based composts that don't have a wetting agent. Most proprietary composts include a wetting

31

agent, but if you're making up your own, it's best to add some at mixing time. You can usually buy wetting agents from larger garden centres or stores.

When cooler, autumnal weather arrives, your plants will need less moisture. In winter you'll rarely need to water outdoor hanging baskets (except, perhaps, after a spell of mild, windy weather) — but if you're keeping plants in the house, or the conservatory, be sure to check them regularly.

Indoor hanging containers are usually small and light enough to take down at watering time. Even so, it's best to use the ones with built-in or clip-on drip trays; this avoids ruining furniture and carpets! Self-watering containers are also useful, for similar reasons, and especially for plants that are too large to take down every time you want to water them.

Watering hanging baskets by hand is often a chilly job — especially if you're standing underneath, with the watering can above your head. If you've

got a number of hanging baskets to deal with, use a step ladder. That way there's less risk of soaking yourself instead of the plants. If heights bother you, you could invest in some specialised watering equipment.

There are some excellent hosepipe lance attachments available, and these come with adjustable flow controls. One type delivers the water through a conventional spray head; a more recent model has a lance that's curved at the end. This allows you to put water directly into the compost, where it's needed most. Another variant has a pump-action watering device that holds about a litre of water — very useful if only a few baskets need attention.

Most experts agree that in summer plants prefer to be watered slowly in the evening or at night — and watering by hand can be a time-consuming job, especially if you have a large collection. I have used several different drip irrigation methods to soak hanging and wall baskets outside.

A do-it-yourself watering system

One of the simplest DIY methods I have seen can be made from any plastic soft drink bottle (larger sizes are ideal for large, well-stocked baskets) and a special on/off watering nozzle. Drill a hole just big enough to take the water delivery tube in the bottom of the bottle, and fix the tube in place with a spot of superglue.

Make a hook out of strong wire, and twist the other end securely round the neck of the bottle. Fill the bottle with water (or liquid feed) and hang it over the basket by hooking it on the support bracket in the evening. The base of the bottle should be level with the surface of the compost.

Switch the nozzle to the 'on' position, and adjust it to give a fast or slow drip rate. I like this method because the whole device can be taken down — and away — in the morning!

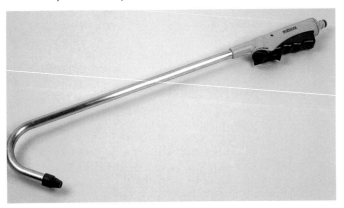

The Hozelock Basket Lance features a curved delivery tube and adjustable flow control.

Holiday times can pose problems for the hanging basket enthusiast, especially if there's nobody on hand to do the watering. However, several specialist companies offer partly or fully automatic drip irrigation systems that take care of the job while you're at work, or on holiday.

These systems need to be connected to an outside mains water supply. You can turn them on and off by hand, or make them semi-automatic by installing a flow control meter. This will turn off the water after a predetermined volume has been delivered.

For complete automation, link the mains supply to a battery-powered timing device. These so-called 'water computers' are rather expensive, but ideal for switching the system on and off at pre-set times while you're lazing in the sun. Another worthwhile piece of wizardry is an override that will stop the system switching on if it's been raining!

Most amateur trickle irrigation kits work allow for reduced water pressure in summer. They come complete with a pressure regulator to maintain the right pressure at all times. Without this the system is liable to blow apart as mains water pressure increases.

Most systems will also feature an in-line water filter to reduce the risk of nozzle blockage, though in hard water areas you may still need to clean them periodically. I clean my system 5

(Above) Drip irrigation systems like this one can be turned on by hand, or fully automated by connecting the supply hose to a battery-powered timing device or computer.

(Right) Drip or trickle irrigation lines usually incorporate an in-line filter and water pressure regulator.

The single most important factor in getting the best out of your hanging baskets is probably correct watering.

Hose essentials

- Before connecting irrigation systems or hand-held watering lances to the mains, make sure a double check valve has been fitted to the outside tap. This is now a legal requirement: failure to install one could result in a hefty fine.
- If your mains supply is not metered, you must apply for a hose licence if you're installing trickle irrigation systems. You don't need a licence for hand-held watering equipment such as hose lance attachments.
- Before watering your baskets with hose attachments or trickle irrigation systems, check with your local water company whether a hosepipe ban is in operation.

nozzles by dipping them in vinegar for a few minutes, then using a piece of fuse wire to clear away stubborn deposits.

As a rough guide, two trickle feed watering nozzles should be enough to serve a medium-sized hanging basket.

General maintenance

Watering and feeding are the most important regular jobs you'll need to do, and will ensure steady plant growth — but there's more to do if you want to keep your basket display in tip-top condition.

Dead-heading (removing faded flowers) is essential if you want the longest possible display period. If you allow plants to set seed they'll divert valuable resources away from growth and flower production. In extreme cases they could simply collapse.

My own policy is to dead-head any faded flowers I notice while I'm watering the baskets. That's usually enough for indoor displays, and for outdoor displays in winter and spring, but in summer I check all the baskets at least once a week.

When you're dead-heading, remove any dead, badly faded, or damaged foliage at the same time. If they're left on the plant they'll spoil the look of your display — but they could also allow disease to set in. Keep an eye open for the first signs of pest or disease problems, and apply a suitable pesticide promptly. Aphids, red spider mites and white flies are the most common basket plant pests, and powdery mildew is the commonest disease.

Be careful if you're spraying high-level baskets, and do it when there is little or no wind and the basket is not exposed to direct sunlight. And don't stand where spray drift will fall back on you!

From time to time you may need to pinch back unduly vigorous growth that threatens to swamp neighbouring plants and unbalance the display. Where possible, it pays to turn the baskets: this encourages even plant growth and flowering.

In very severe weather, winter and spring display baskets will benefit from temporary protection in a cold greenhouse or a porch. Otherwise put them in a shed or garage, as long as they can get some light.

Summer display baskets may also need temporary protection if late frost is forecast. If you can, it's best to move them under cover. If you can't, cover the whole basket with newspaper or proprietary horticultural fleece in the evening.

A subtle mixture of colours produced by red fuchsias, pink busy lizzies and ivy-leaved geraniums, plus a generous helping of blue and white lobelias.

Flowering shrubs

Hanging baskets offer rather limited growing space, so your choice of summer flowering shrubs tends to be rather restricted. However, by choosing shrubs that have a naturally dwarf habit, or selecting varieties that can be kept within practical bounds by hard annual pruning, it's possible to achieve quite spectacular results.

Most flowering shrubs that fall within these categories are tender: they'll need protection from cold in the winter. Several are half-hardy: these can safely be overwintered in a frost-free greenhouse or conservatory. The more exotic plants from the tropics should be taken indoors, where conditions will be warmer.

Fuchsias
Fuchsia cultivars

This popular group of hardy and half-hardy shrubs provides a staggering selection of varieties. The most suitable tend to display arching or trailing growth habits, and as well as single, semi-double and double blooms, many also provide the bonus of attractive foliage colours.

Display: Fuchsias are usually very free-flowering, and they're one of the best choices for creating single plant displays in free-hanging or wall-supported baskets. Flowering is usually continuous throughout summer and early autumn.

Site: Partial to full shade. For best results, site double-flowered varieties in the most sheltered positions possible.

Cultural tips: For preference use young plants in 3½ in (9 cm) pots. To encourage a well-clothed basket, pinch out growing tips of shoots when three or four pairs of leaves have developed.

Keep a careful watch for whiteflies and aphids throughout the growing season, and control with a suitable insecticide as directed on the label.

Varieties: Several strains are now available as seeds, including Fl hybrid 'Florabelle'. Named varieties raised by means of cuttings include: 'Dancing Flame' a recent double orange-flowered type; 'La Campanella', a floriferous semi-double variety with a purple corolla and pink-flushed, white sepals; 'Golden Marinka', with rich red flowers and variegated foliage; 'Pink Marshmallow' with large, pink blooms; and deep rose and crimson 'Red Spider', with narrow, recurving sepals.

Fuchsia 'Florabella'

Weeping Chinese lantern
Abutilon megapotamicon

A. megapotamicon is a half-hardy trailing species suitable for large baskets. The leaves are arrow-shaped and about 3 in (7.5 cm) long. The small red and yellow lantern-like blooms are produced on slender, weeping stems. In milder regions this deciduous species can be overwintered in a sheltered spot outside, or in a cold greenhouse if you keep the compost fairly dry.

Display: A succession of flowers all summer into early autumn. *A. megapotamicon* 'Variegatum' has yellow mottled leaves.

Site: A well-lit or partially shaded spot is preferable.

Cultural tips: Feed regularly throughout the summer. Prune back shoots by about half their length in late autumn to ensure a bushy plant the following year.
   Sow seeds or take stem cuttings in spring. Variegated forms must be propagated by cuttings.

Red-hot cat's tail
Acalypha hispida

A. hispida is a rather large, upright plant more suited to a warm greenhouse, but its variety 'Hispaniola' is a compact, trailing form well suited to basket plantings. In cooler regions this one is best confined to sheltered spots under glass, but in milder southern and

Above: Weeping Chinese lantern (Abutilon megapotamicon).

Right: Red-hot cat's tail (Acalypha hispida)

western counties of Britain it can be tried outdoors during the summer months.
   Plants are available from a few specialists offering collections of basket fillers, and from suppliers of exotics.

Display: A floriferous form of cat's tail covered with crimson-pink tassels during summer.

Removal of spent flower heads is essential to promote continuous flowering.

Site: A warm, sheltered site is necessary for this plant. It requires good light, but avoid prolonged exposure to direct sun. In autumn move plants into a warm room indoors, or a heated conservatory.

Cultural tips: This plant revels in warm, moist air conditions. Mist overhead regularly in warm weather and keep a sharp watch for signs of red spider mite.

Prune back shoots by about half their length in late summer or spring. Propagate by taking cuttings in spring.

Centradenia

An unusual tropical evergreen from Mexico that has only recently become generally available. *C. inaeguilateralis* 'Cascade' is the plant normally offered, and it has attractive burnished bronze foliage produced on trailing stems reaching about 1 ft (30 cm) in height.

Plants are occasionally offered by suppliers of exotics, and in unusual basket collections.

Display: This species is grown mainly for its foliage display, since its main flowering time is winter. However, the occasional flat, cerise-coloured flowers may be seen in spring and summer.

Site: Sheltered spot in good indirect light. In cooler regions it's best seen as a basket plant for the home or conservatory.

Cultural tips: Needs overwintering in a warm room or heated conservatory. Propagate by rooting side-shoot cuttings in late winter or early spring, in warmth.

Centradenia inaeguilateralis *'Cascade'*

Lantana

Lantana montevidensis

This vigorous-growing shrub is suitable for larger baskets. Most widely offered is the bushy *L. camara* (yellow sage), with rather coarse leaves and dense clusters of verbena-like flowers (irresistible to butterflies!)

Named varieties include 'Mine d'Ore' (golden yellow), 'Brazier' (bright red touched with orange), 'Feston Rose' (pink and yellow), and low-growing types such as 'Carpet Yellow' and 'Carpet Orange'.

L. montevidensis is a spreading plant with downy foliage, particularly suited to both indoor and outdoor baskets. It bears flattish heads of rosy-lilac flowers; other named forms include 'Snow Queen' (white), 'Malan's Gold' (rosy-violet flowers over yellow foliage) and 'Aloha' (yellow flowers over yellow variegated foliage).

Display: In ideal conditions these plants are prolific. *L. camara* will give a brilliant display from spring until the first frost, and if you move *L. montevidensis* to a warm conservatory in early autumn it will continue to flower into winter.

Site: Good light, but ideally slightly shaded from direct noonday sun in summer.

Cultural tips: Treat rather like a fuchsia — pinch out tips of shoots to encourage bushiness. In autumn, lightly prune back any plants you want to keep for the following year, and overwinter in a minimum temperature of 40°F (4°C). Hard prune in early spring to encourage new growth.

Propagate by sowing seeds in late winter, or by soft cuttings in late spring and early summer.

Roses
Rosa cultivars

Perhaps not an obvious choice for baskets, but several modern low-growing ground-cover varieties can be used to unusual effect in large containers.

The 'County' series includes several useful varieties, some growing up to 20 in (50 cm) tall and others up to 40 in (1 m). These include the fragrant, double-flowered 'Gwent' (yellow), the slightly fragrant single-flowered 'Hertfordshire' (carmine pink), and the slightly fragrant single-flowered 'Suffolk' (scarlet).

'Magic Carpet' is another good variety for large baskets, as the spicy-perfumed, semi-double, lavender flowers are borne all along the arching branches.

Display: All the ground cover varieties mentioned are floriferous and repeat flowering, giving a display throughout the summer.

Site: A sheltered, sunny position is best to ensure continuous flowering.

Cultural hints: Ground-cover roses need a container at least 12 in (30 cm) deep. A soil-based compost is preferable, but soilless mixes can be used if you feed the plants regularly throughout the growing and flowering season.

Above: *Rose 'Nozomi' in a half-basket*

Right: *The County series of rose varieties, such as single-flowered 'Hertfordshire', make an unusual short-term solo plant for hanging containers and wall tubs.*

Half-hardy flowers

Almost all the popular half-hardy summer bedding plants can be used to furnish a hanging basket. However, those with a particularly vigorous growth habit may not be suitable for small containers, so it's usually a good idea to check on the eventual height and spread of varieties before you buy.

There are also a number of less familiar plants that make excellent container material, though many are only available as plants from garden centres or by mail order. Quite often the most unusual subjects aren't easy to track down as individual plants, but form part of a special basket collection. However, you can propagate most of them at home by means of cuttings or division, so you should be able to build up your own stock over one or two seasons.

Bacopa

Also listed as *Sutera*, this useful small-leaved plant produces a continuous stream of small, musk-shaped flowers. The variety 'Snowflake' is widely available and useful for its compact, trailing habit. This mat-forming variety is liberally sprinkled with white blooms; other varieties include 'Pink Domino' and the more upright growing 'Knysna Hills', with lavender-coloured blooms. *Bacopa* is available in a form suitable for mixed plantings, or you can use it as a solo subject in small hanging baskets or wall pots.

Begonias
Begonia hybrids

These floriferous perennials make superb material for all types of hanging container. The fibrous-rooted Semperflorens group make dense, compact plants that associate well with other plants of open growth, whereas the more vigorous tuberous-rooted types often look best on their own.

Fibrous-rooted Begonia semperflorens *comes in red, pink and white flowering forms and has attractive green or bronze-purple foliage.*

Semperflorens begonias are available in a wide range of varieties with single red, pink or white flowers. These include Fl hybrid mixtures such as 'Cocktail', 'Organdy' and 'Ambassador'. As well as their flower display, many Semperflorens varieties offer the bonus of glossy, ornate foliage in shades of burnished bronze, reddish-purple or green.

The so-called Pendula or trailing begonias are particularly well suited to basket display. Older tuberous varieties tend to have rather small, narrow-petalled flowers, but modern varieties are larger and much more prolific. Types to try include the large-flowered, fully double Sensation series, available in clear red, pink, orange, yellow and white, or trailing types such as 'Musical Yellow' and 'Musical Scarlet'.

You'll normally discard Semperflorens begonias at the end of each season, but you can keep the tuberous-rooted types for further displays over a number of years. Gradually reduce the frequency of your watering; this will encourage top growth to fade and die back in autumn. Then store the dry tubers in a cool, frostproof place until the following spring.

Bidens 'Golden Goddess'

Bidens

Although rather sprawling in habit, this sun-loving plant is ideal for interplanting in denser material. The slender stems bear finely cut foliage and many yellow, star-shaped flowers. *B. ferulifolia* is widely available, but look out for the variety 'Golden Goddess' with bright yellow blooms and attractive dark-green foliage.

Although perennial, *Bidens* is usually treated as a half-hardy annual and discarded each year. It's very easy to grow from seeds sown in warmth during late winter or early spring.

Swan River daisy
Brachycome iberidifolia

This half-hardy annual is widely available both as plants and seeds. These fine-leaved and bushy plants grow up to about 12 in (30 cm) tall, and produce a continuous succession of small, daisy-like blooms from late spring onwards. Seed mixtures contain blue-, pink- and white-flowered forms, but for separate colours try varieties such as 'Blue Star' and 'White Splendour'.

There are also several perennial sorts that are suitable for hanging baskets. The following varieties are occasionally offered in mail-order basket collections, or as individual items from specialist suppliers: 'Pink Mist' (mauve-pink), 'Lemon Mist' (soft yellow), 'Misty Blue' and 'Harmony' (purple). All grow up to about 8 in (20 cm) tall.

Brachycome revels in a sheltered, sunny spot. As growth can be semi-trailing, it's suitable for side positions in baskets, or as a top filler.

Swan river daisy (Brachycome)

Slipper flower
Calceolaria

C. integrifolia (syn. *C. rugosa*) yields a prolific mass of small, yellow, pouch-like flowers throughout the summer. Young plants will soon grow up to 10 in (25 cm) tall, and despite their vigorous habit they rarely overshadow other plants.

Slipper flowers make superb flower fillers on the sides or the top of baskets, and they're equally successful in sun or light shade.

They're available as plants in larger garden centres, or you can raise your own from seeds sown in late winter or early spring. Seed varieties include Fl hybrid 'Midas' and 'Sunshine'.

You can root soft shoot-tip cuttings in summer, and over-winter the resultant plants in a frost-free greenhouse or conservatory.

Diascia

Much interest has been shown in this superb group of African plants, and many are proving remarkably hardy. Both upright and low-growing types are available, giving plenty of scope for all-round basket planting. Heights of the varieties mentioned below range from 3 in (7.5 cm) to 12 in (30 cm), with spreads of 9–24 in (23–60 cm).

Diascias produce a profusion of small, bell-shaped flowers throughout the summer, mainly in shades of pink, but breeding has produced a range of coral, apricot and lavender. Plants are readily available from garden centres and by mail order, and at least one variety is offered as seeds, which should be sown in warmth during late winter or early spring.

The list of varieties is large, and increases annually, but the following are considered fairly winter-hardy in Britain:

'Blackthorn Apricot' is a modest grower bearing pale apricot flowers; 'Lady Valerie' is low-growing with salmon-pink flowers; 'Lilac Belle' has lilac-pink flowers; 'Lilac Mist' is a cascading plant with soft lavender blooms; and 'Ruby Field' is a well-known sort with pink flowers. Seed varieties include 'Pink Queen', with dark-centred pink bells.

Diascias produce a prolific crop of delicate, bell-shaped flowers in a range of pink, coral, apricot and lavender shades.

Blue daisy
Felicia amelloides

This sun-loving plant produces rather open, cascading growth that is suitable for combination planting with other basket plants of moderate vigour. The bright blue daisy-like flowers are the main attraction, but in the variety 'Variegata' the creamy-yellow markings on the foliage are a bonus.

Both the species and its variegated form are widely offered as plants, but some selected types to look out for include 'Read's White' and 'Santa Anita', the latter bearing larger than usual blue flowers. These grow up to around 12 in (30 cm) tall and as much, or more, across.

Lobelia
Lobelia erinus

Lobelia is one of the mainstays of summer bedding, and ideal for smothering the sides of baskets with colour, especially in partial shade. The flowers are usually small, but they appear in abundance. Varieties that display a spreading or trailing habit are particularly useful for baskets.

The following selection may be obtained as seeds (and some as plants) from garden centres or by mail order. Colour mixtures include 'Cascade Mixed' and 'Fountains Mixed' — the latter contains shades of blue, lilac, rose, crimson and white. Separate colours are available from both these series, to which you can add white-eyed, blue-flowered 'Sapphire Trailing' and 'Regatta Marine'.

Lobelias form generous concentrations of bloom, and are especially useful for hiding the sides of baskets. Here they have been crowned by a pink Diascia.

As well as the types raised from seed, look out for two sterile varieties: double-flowered 'Kathleen Mallard' and the wide-spreading plant offered as *L. richardsonii*. The former is a prolific, bushy plant with delightful, fully double, blue flowers that often obscure the foliage. The latter has larger, deep-blue blooms borne on relatively thick dark-green stems. Both can be overwintered in a frost-free place and are propagated by taking cuttings in early spring or autumn.

Nemesia

A host of brilliantly coloured, half-hardy annual hybrid varieties are offered both as seeds and plants. Most have rather slender stems, so they're good as fillers or in top positions for baskets in sunny situations.

Flamboyant mixtures, like 'Funfair' and 'Tapestry', can be used, but if you're trying to colour co-ordinate your plantings you'll get the best effects with selected colours. Typical varieties include 'Blue Gem', a bushy sort growing up to 10 in (25 cm), and 'Mellow White', reaching 7-9 in (18-23 cm).

Perennial species also provide desirable selections and hybrids to complement other basket plants. Perennial nemesias give a long, prolific display of purple, pink, lilac or white flowers on slender growth reaching about 1 ft (30 cm) tall.

Larger garden centres usually stock one or two sorts, but you may need to track down the

Selected seed-raised plants and named varieties can readily be increased using side-shoot cuttings rooted in early autumn. Carefully remove any flower stems, and trim shoots down to 2–3 in (5–7.5 cm), trimming them squarely under a convenient leaf joint with a sharp blade. Remove lower leaves and place cuttings on a greenhouse bench or an indoor window-sill overnight. This will allow the wounded surface to dry. Remaining leaves may wilt slightly, but this should not prove a problem. Insert cuttings into well-drained compost or Jiffy 7s and root in moderate warmth (cold greenhouse temperatures should suffice). Rooted cuttings should be moved into small pots and overwintered in a frost-free greenhouse, conservatory or cool room indoors.

scarcer varieties in mail-order lists from specialist nurseries. *N. fruticans* 'Joan Wilder' has blue-lilac flowers, 'Woodcote' has purple blooms with a yellow eye, 'Innocence' bears white flowers, and the plant offered as *N. denticulata* has flowers in shades of pale pink.

If you want to grow your own nemesias sow the annual sorts in March, or take cuttings of perennial types in autumn or spring.

Geranium *Pelargonium* hybrids

Several groups of this popular summer plant have proved ideally suited to hanging basket displays, but all of them need a sunny situation to encourage floriferous, sturdy growth.

The trailing ivy-leaved varieties are especially suited to hanging baskets, and both plain and variegated-leaved forms are

A mixed planting of red ivy-leaved geraniums, lobelias and yellow French marigolds.

available. Most are offered as plants, but Fl hybrid 'Summer Showers' is also available as seeds that should be sown in heat during early autumn or spring.

Older varieties of ivy-leaved geranium include 'La France', a semi-double lilac with maroon markings, 'L'Elégante', a purple-streaked single white with white-edged grey-green leaves, and 'Sybil Holmes', a more compact type that produces dark-red, semi-double blooms.

The well known Cascade or Balcon type, seen everywhere in the European Alps, is now more readily available as plants, and these are ideal on their own or in combination with other basket plants. There is also a scarce variegated-leaf form of the red Balcon type, plus superb, extra-floriferous dwarf varieties offered as Mini Cascades.

Some zonal geraniums, such as the fancy or coloured-leaf variety 'Frank Headley', are also useful for centre planting on the tops of baskets, but take care not to choose over-vigorous varieties that would unbalance the effect. 'Frank Headley' is particularly suitable, as it is rather dwarf and produces lax growth covered with white-variegated foliage. The flowers are single and pink in colour.

Another lesser-known group that make superb solo basket plants are the Angels, an attractive small-flowered group of regal pelargoniums. These compact, bushy plants must usually be obtained from mail-order specialist growers. Varieties include white-and-rose 'Mrs G. H. Smith'; 'Spanish Angel', with dark picotee-edged upper petals; and light-edged, plum-purple 'Velvet Duet'.

Surfinia petunias make vigorous, prolific plants with a cascading habit.

Prolific petunias

Fl hybrid varieties to try from seeds sown in early spring include the Fl hybrid Super Cascade series, a floriferous single Grandiflora type sold as a mixture or in single-colour selections such as blue, lilac, salmon and white; double-flowered Multiflora 'Duo Mixed'; or clear lavender-pink double 'Heavenly lavender'. For spectacular trailing effects, try single-flowered 'Purple Wave', in brilliant purple with a dark throat, or 'Pink Wave', with a slightly denser growth habit and white-throated flowers. The more compact, small-flowered Milliflora or Junior petunias make good solo plants for small baskets, or top-edge plantings in mixed baskets. Available as the Fantasy series, these grow up to 4 in (10 cm) tall in a wide range of colours. Varieties available only as plants include vigorous, single-flowered, cascading types like the Surfinia petunias, and less familiar sorts, e.g. the Born Free series and the double-flowered 'Able Mabel'. The diminutive-flowered Million Bells series is another unusual addition to the 'basket brigade', but only a sheltered spot will encourage maximum results from this very prolific petunia.

Petunia
Petunia hybrids

This popular, sun-loving plant has been much improved in recent years. Many more colour combinations have been introduced, and many of the new strains are rather more tolerant of poor weather conditions.

Trailing varieties are particularly valuable for planting in hanging baskets, but some upright types are also useful for top centre positions.

Petunias are very prolific and make superb material for solo planting, but they are just as effective when you use them in association with other plants.

The choice of seed varieties is very wide, and gives you the option of single or double flower forms. Doubles give a very dramatic show, but faded flowers tend to persist, and if not removed they can mar the overall effect. Flower size is now very variable, ranging from the large Grandifloras down to the diminutive Millifloras.

However, in recent years many new varieties have been developed specifically for displaying in hanging baskets and other containers. These are propagated by means of cuttings, and they are widely offered by garden centres and mail-order companies.

Some of these varieties make very large cascading plants, and again you will find that both double and single flower forms are available.

Fan flower
Scaevola aemula

This unusual half-hardy perennial produces vigorous prostrate shoots which take on a semi-trailing character as they grow clear of the basket. Each shoot terminates in dense clusters of white-eyed, blue flowers that have a vaguely fan-shaped appearance.

It associates well with dense and bushy subjects, as the shoots grow through to display their flowers well away from the basket, but solo plantings of this sun-loving plant can create quite a stunning effect.

Vigorous young plants offered as 'Blue Wonder' and 'Blue Fan' are widely available, and occasionally the white-flowered form 'Alba' appears in specialist mail-order catalogues.

The fan flower can be increased by rooting stem cuttings in a heated propagator during autumn or spring.

*F1 hybrid 'Pink Wave' (**top**) is a vigorous, spreading petunia that has proved ideal for baskets and other containers.*

*Fan flower Scaevola aemula (**above**)*

49

Black-eyed Susan
Thunbergia alata

This vigorous climbing annual produces slender stems clothed in rather bristly small leaves and a multitude of flowers from early summer until autumn. It prefers a sheltered position and revels in good light.

The typical plant has orange flowers punctuated by an almost black middle or 'eye', but occasionally the 'eyeless' *T. a. gibsonii* occurs in batches of seedlings. Other colour forms occur naturally, and these have been used to produce 'Susie', a modern hybrid mixture that gives a succession of orange, yellow and white flowers, with or without dark 'eyes'.

Grown as a climber, both the species and its hybrids can reach up to 4 ft (1.2 m) in height, which makes them ideal for disguising supporting chains and brackets, as well as for trailing over and down the sides

Black-eyed Susan (Thunbergia alata) *is a half-hardy climber, ideal for camouflaging the supporting chains of hanging baskets.*

of baskets. Black-eyed Susan makes an ideal subject for solo planting in baskets, but in a mixed collection it's perhaps best to restrict it to a single individual (ideally climbing the chains) to avoid other plants being overwhelmed.

The less well known *T. fragrans* has somewhat larger, yellow-centred, white blooms that are lightly perfumed. Although perennial, it is usually treated as an annual and used in exactly the same fashion as black-eyed Susan.

You won't often come across *T. fragrans*, but seeds are sometimes sold under the varietal name 'Angel Wings'. *T. alata*, however, is widely available in seed form and as a mature plant from garden centres.

Verbena × *hybrida*

Many varieties of hybrid verbena are available, but the lax or spreading sorts are best for hanging baskets. Most verbenas prefer sunny conditions, but some will tolerate a little light shade for part of the day.

Hybrid verbenas fall into two main categories: those raised from seeds sown in heat during early spring, and named forms, which are propagated from cuttings rooted in autumn and overwintered in a frost-free greenhouse or conservatory.

Seed varieties to look out for include 'Imagination', a rather lax-growing type that produces abundant narrow spikes of small, deep blue-violet flowers, and 'Showtime', an excellent mixture giving larger flower heads in shades of purple, violet, red, pink and white.

Notable named forms of verbena offered as plants include varieties such as the fine-leaved, magenta-pink 'Sissinghurst'; red 'Lawrence Johnston'; 'Aphrodite', purple with white stripes; powder-blue 'Blue Knight' and its white counterpart 'White Knight'; fragrant, pink bicolour 'Pink Parfait'; and equally fragrant, silvery-pink 'Silver Anne'.

A recent addition to the list is the extra-prolific 'Tapien', which makes tightly knit growth topped by large heads of violet-purple flowers. This variety looks particularly effective on its own, or you can use it in combination with other plants.

Ten unusual types

Asarina is a group of slender climbing perennials bearing numerous small trumpet or snapdragon flowers in shades of violet, red, pink and white. Plants listed under this name include the chicabiddy, *A. scandens* (syn. *Maurandia scandens*), *A. barclaiana* (syn. *M. barclaiana*), *A. erubescens* (syn. *M. erubescens*), and *A. antirrhiniflora*.

Suitable for sunny or partially shaded positions. Ideal to trail over the edges of baskets, or to train up supporting chains and brackets. Widely available as seed mixtures or single colours like purple 'Victoria Falls'. Sow in early spring.

Several **snapdragon** (*Antirrhinum*) selections can make unusual basket subjects. 'Avalanche' is a cascading variety with trailing shoots clothed in grey-green foliage and delicate white flowers. 'Lampion' does not trail so obviously, but is more floriferous and comes in a wide range of colours, including self-coloured and bicoloured flowers.

Young plants of these sun-loving trailing antirrhinums are available from larger garden centres and by mail order.

Camissonia is an unusual annual that has only recently become available as seeds.

'Sunflakes' is one of the varieties offered; it makes slender spreading stems 8–12 in (20–30 cm) long, each bearing small, brilliant-yellow blooms like miniature evening primroses.

This sun-loving, drought-resistant annual is suitable for top planting as a filler with other moderate-growing plants, or positioned where it can spill over the edge of baskets.

*Unusual trailing antirrhinum 'Avalanche' (**top**) is widely offered in mail order hanging basket plant collections. Camissonia 'Sunflakes' (**right**) resembles a miniature, sprawling evening primrose; it's available as seeds in several mail order lists.*

Lysimachia congestifolia *'Outback Sunset'* has yellow variegated foliage.

Lysimachia: The floriferous plant offered as *L. congestifolia* makes a substantial trailing specimen clothed in dark, broad leaves and attractive globular heads of red-throated, yellow flowers. Also offered as *L. lyssii*, named selections include 'Golden Falls' and 'Outback Sunset', the latter notable for its yellow variegated foliage.

Lysimachias will grow in full sun or partial shade, and relish moist growing conditions. They're available as young plants in spring, and can be propagated by means of division or cuttings.

The **yellow lobelia** (*Monopsis lutea*) is a curious perennial, occasionally offered as plants from mail-order specialists. The canary-yellow, hooded flowers are borne at the tips of spreading stems that reach no more than 8 in (20 cm) in height.

The yellow lobelia is a South African marsh-dweller that prefers a sunny position and plenty of moisture.

The **Chilean bellflower** (*Nolana paradoxa*) is an easy annual producing numerous trailing stems liberally dotted with 2 in (5 cm) wide, upward-facing trumpet flowers all summer. The plants can tolerate

The **rock isotome** (*Solenopsis*), also listed as *Isotoma* and *Laurentia*, makes 1 ft (30 cm) tall bushy plants, which in summer become liberally sprinkled with clear-blue starry flowers. The rather dense mass of fine foliage makes this an excellent filler plant, but beware bruising the foliage, as the sap may cause irritation.

S. axillaris, both in the typical blue-flowered form and the less familiar white selection, is widely offered as plants and seeds. A pink form is also occasionally offered as plants from specialist mail-order suppliers.

This perennial plant prefers some shade. Seeds must be sown very early to ensure a good summer display. Cuttings may be taken in summer (avoid getting the sap on your skin) and the resultant plants can be overwintered in a heated conservatory or greenhouse.

quite dry conditions and prefer a sunny situation.

Sow seeds of the blue-flowered variety 'Bluebird' or the white-flowered 'Snowbird' in spring. Both sorts grow up to about 6 in (15 cm) tall.

The near-hardy **blue shamrock pea** (*Parochetus communis*) makes long, trailing growth that looks most impressive when allowed to spill over the edges of baskets. This perennial produces a late show of vivid blue, pea-like flowers and is occasionally offered in collections of basket plants. Individual plants are also available from mail-order specialists.

The blue shamrock pea is happy in sun or shade, but plenty of moisture is essential during the growing season. Established plants will often overwinter outdoors, but it pays to take cuttings or pot up rooted pieces in autumn and move these under glass.

The low-growing **perennial knotweed** (*Persicaria capitata*), formerly known as *Polygonum capitatum*, makes slender spreading growth about 6 in (15 cm) tall. It produces attractive green leaves that are marked with dark V-shaped bands, and bears numerous small globular heads of pink flowers from July onwards.

The yellow lobelia (Monopsis lutea) *needs good light and plenty of moisture.*

This useful plant is ideal for solo planting in small baskets, or as a top- or side-trailing subject in combination displays. It roots readily at the leaf axils and you can easily increase it by means of shoot cuttings in summer. Available as plants, sometimes under the varietal name 'Pink Bubbles'.

The **sun plant** (*Portulaca grandiflora*) is a delightful half-hardy annual succulent that will give its best display in full sun. It's especially useful where baskets tend to dry out rapidly. It makes a good solo plant for small hanging containers, or can be planted at the sides of baskets to take advantage of its semi-trailing growth habit. Most

strains reach up to around 6 in (15 cm) in height.

Plants are offered by larger garden centres in late spring, and solo planted hanging containers are often available in summer. Alternatively you can raise your own from seeds sown in warmth during early spring.

Modern seed strains include double-flowered 'Cloudbeater Mixed'; unlike older strains, this one doesn't close up in cloudy conditions. Colours include pink, red, white, yellow, and pink-flushed creamy-yellow. Other varieties include pure-white double-flowered 'Swanlake', and Fl hybrid 'Sundial Peppermint', with magenta-flecked pale-pink flowers.

Hardy flowers

Compared to the wide range of tender plants suitable for hanging baskets, the choice of hardy summer flowering subjects may appear very restricted. Yet those that are available provide a display equal to the majority of their tender kin, and a few are unsurpassed in their profusion of blooms.

You can use them with half-hardy flowering shrubs and bedding subjects — or in the case of the vigorous prolific varieties, you can treat them as special interest solo plants.

Most plants in this category are treated as annuals, and if you want to raise your own plants, you can usually do it by sowing seeds under glass in late winter or early spring. Such plants are then discarded at the end of each flowering season.

However, you can keep some of the perennial subjects so that you'll have a display in the following year. Generally it's best to pot up the plants in autumn, then overwinter them in a cold frame or greenhouse. Alternatively, there are a small number that are best propagated by taking cuttings in early autumn and overwintering rooted youngsters under cover.

Giant blue pimpernel
Anagallis monellii

Related to our native scarlet pimpernel, this Mediterranean species produces large flowers in the most stunning shade of vivid blue. Plants are occasionally offered in mail-order catalogues, but seeds are a better alternative if you need a lot of plants.

The blue pimpernel makes bushy plants that can be up to about 9 in (23 cm) tall, and in good growing conditions on a sunny site the foliage may be almost obscured by the sheer profusion of flowers. Individual flowers reach around $\frac{3}{4}$ in (2 cm) across, and are produced in succession from spring through to the first hard frost.

Campanula carpatica

This low-growing perennial bellflower is one of the most prolific species, and modern Fl hybrid varieties give a display equal to any half-hardy bedding subject. Plants are widely available in spring, or seeds may be sown early in the year to give flowering plants in May.

Of the many varieties available, Fl hybrid 'Bellissimo' is notable for its profusion of white or blue chalice-shaped blooms. Individual flowers may be up to 2 in (5 cm) across, and they grow in profusion on plants that reach no more than 6 in (15 cm) or so in height. Use this bell-flower for solo planting in small baskets, or as a filler.

Convolvulus sabatius

Formerly listed as *C. mauritanicus*, this blue-flowered trailing plant is ideal in a mixed basket in full sun. Most plants have pale-blue flowers, but a dark-blue form is sometimes offered, and pink forms are occasionally found.

Plants are available by mail order, from specialist nurseries

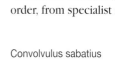

Convolvulus sabatius

and from larger garden centres. Use them to supplement more vigorous fillers in the sides and tops of baskets.

This species is perfectly hardy in milder districts; given the protection of a cold greenhouse or frame, most plants will overwinter without too much trouble. However, it pays to take cuttings in autumn as an insurance.

Florists' chrysanthemum
Dendranthema cultivars

Dwarf or miniature varieties of the popular florists' chrysanthemum are ideal for providing a display of colour from late summer until the first frosts. In many cases the plants seen at garden centres will be artificially dwarfed, but this will not detract from their welcome display.

The Carnival series is very attractive, with a profusion of double, button-like flowers about the size of a ten pence coin. Colours include white, yellow and red on plants about 12 in (30 cm) tall. Use them as solo plants, or in combination with slender-growing trailers in good light.

Carnation
Dianthus caryophyllus

Often designated as half-hardy, several of the modern Fl hybrid carnations have proved very tolerant of British winters. In addition, the Continental Swiss

The Carnival range of miniature chrysanthemum (Dendranthema cultivars) makes an eye-catching display in late summer and autumn.

Balcony or Trailing strains, in shades of red and pink, are ideal subjects for summer hanging baskets.

Plants are occasionally offered in spring. Seeds are available from several companies and should be sown early in the year in a heated propagator. Plant at the top edge of baskets and put in a sunny position.

Gypsophila muralis

A much-branched slender annual species growing 6–10 in (15–25 cm) tall. It produces a profusion of dainty, veined, pink flowers from July to October. *Gypsophila* is ideal as a light-weight filler in sun, and tolerates fairly dry conditions.

Seeds offered under the name of 'Garden Bride' are best sown in mid-spring.

Sweet pea
Lathyrus odoratus

Provided the seed pods are regularly removed, the dwarf, semi-trailing strains of this popular hardy annual make a novel addition to hanging baskets. Garden centres sometimes offer plants in spring, but the best way to ensure a supply of these dwarf varieties is to raise your own from seeds sown in late winter or early spring. Seeds sown under cover from January to March will start flowering from June to July.

Of the varieties available, the recent 'Fantasia' is possibly the most suitable for hanging baskets. This little beauty makes compact growth and produces a mass of small flowers in a good colour range. Other useful sorts include the pink-flowered 'Cupid', 'Snoopea' and 'Bijou'. Try them as solo plants, or as top or side fillers in medium or large baskets in a sunny situation.

Nemophila menziesii
Seeds of this little-known dainty annual should be sown in March or early April. It makes a spreading plant about 4 in (10 cm)

high, and its non-smothering filigree of foliage makes an attractive foil for the numerous bowl-shaped blooms.

The selection offered as 'Pennie Black' has unusual and attractive silvery-white flowers sporting dark-purple, almost black centres, while *N. menziesii* var. *atomaria* 'Snowstorm' is a white-flowered form, delicately dotted in black. Use these hardy stunners as semi-trailers around the rims of hanging baskets.

Nodding catchfly
Silene pendula
This attractive carpeting plant can usually be found in larger garden centres, but is readily raised from seeds sown early in the year. The double-flowered varieties are particularly valuable for mixed plantings, and at peak flowering time the foliage may almost disappear beneath a

carpet of $^3/_4$ in (2 cm) wide blooms.

Recent varieties include pure-white 'Snowball' and 'Peach Blossom'. The latter produces a mass of deep-pink buds that open salmon, then gradually fade to white. These plants are ideal for the tops of baskets. A sunny site is preferable.

Globe mallow
Sphaeralcea
A little-known hardy perennial which produces shrubby stems growing 1–2 ft (30–60 cm) long. The mallow-shaped flowers are usually in shades of pink, and measure about 1 in (2.5 cm) across.

Plants of *S. munroana* are now becoming widely available from larger garden centres and specialist mail-order suppliers. Use them as a focal feature for the top-centre positions in baskets. Best in full sun.

Nasturtium
Tropaeolum majus
This common annual is much more versatile than many people realise. The long, trailing habit of traditional sorts is useful for clothing the sides of medium to large baskets, but semi-trailing and compact-growing types make admirable fillers in smaller containers. Their prime use is to provide a wonderful splash of flower colour, but several varieties also offer decorative foliage (see

Nasturtium (Tropaeolum majus)

below). Many delightful strains are available as seeds, including 'Gleam', a semi-trailing mixture in a good range of yellow, orange and red shades. 'Jewel' is a bright semi-double mixture on plants about 9 in (23 cm) tall. For long-ranging trails of foliage liberally interspersed with pale-yellow flowers, try 'Moonlight', a stunning variety with stems that reach 6 ft (1.8 m) in length. Other single-coloured varieties from seeds include compact-growing 'Whirlybird Gold', with deep-yellow single flowers, and 'Peach Melba', a creamy-coloured semi-double, with orange-scarlet central blotches.

Two older varieties, only offered as plants, are the Victorian 'Hermione Grasshof', a wonderful fully double type with bright red-orange blooms, and 'Red Wonder'. The latter is sometimes offered as 'Crimson Beauty', and has beautiful dark-red blooms set against attractive, dark, bronze-purple leaves. Both are trailing types propagated by taking soft cuttings in late winter or early spring.

Violas and pansies
Viola hybrids

The cheerful faces of pansies are a welcome sight at almost any time of the year, but it's the small-flowered viola varieties that look their best in hanging baskets from late spring until autumn. They integrate with other summer-flowering subjects quite readily, but as solo subjects they can be absolutely stunning, especially when

A colourful mixed combination of half-hardy summer bedders set in a wall basket supported by a painted wall.

planted to smother a double basket (globe). Plant at any point in baskets, and site in full sun or partial shade.

Plants are readily available from most garden centres, and numerous varieties are offered as seeds. Miniature pansies are a joy to behold, and varieties to try include the Velour strain, which also come as single-colour selections like 'Purple Velour' and 'Blue Velour'.

The hardy biennial miniature violas are equally attractive, but they can be treated as annuals if sown in gentle warmth during

February or March. Varieties to watch for include 'Bambini Mixed', a superb mixture of pink, apricot, blue, red and violet flowers, all with a distinctive golden centre highlighted with fine dark whiskers. 'Cuty' is reminiscent of the old fashioned heartsease, while 'Alpine Summer' is a glorious blend of lilac and yellow. Other varieties of note are yellow 'Prince John' and purple 'Prince Henry'.

The Princess strain is a development from the perennial *V. cornuta*; at the end of each flowering season plants can be cut back and kept for further displays. Seeds are available, and as well as the mixture you can buy single colours like 'Princess Blue' and 'Princess White'.

57

Foliage fillers

There's no denying that hanging baskets devoted entirely to flower colour can be very eye-catching. Even so, adding a few decorative foliage plants may improve the general effect quite dramatically. Both hardy and tender plants are commonly used for this purpose, and in all but a few cases they are perennial.

Plants displaying prominent leaf variegation are currently very popular for mixed basket combinations. These can be particularly effective when planted with large, self-coloured flowers. Plain-coloured leaves also provide superb backcloths to flowering plants, and many of the most desirable foliage

subjects fall into this category.

In recent years there's been a noticeable increase in the number of new and improved forms of foliage filler. Garden centres and mail-order suppliers offer a host of superb varieties in colours ranging from silvery-white and grey, through muted and glowing yellows, to more unusual hues such as bronze-purple.

The gold-and-green variegated leaves of Lysimachia congestifolia *'Outback Sunset' make a colourful addition in combination with blue brachycome and variegated candle plant (*Plectranthus*)*

However, take care to combine foliage and flowering partners that either contrast with or complement each other. Mixing garishly striped flowers with prominently defined variegated foliage will inevitably produce an awful, clashing result that will certainly mar the whole effect.

As well as decorative leaf colour, pleasing foliage textures and ornate shapes can also enhance the overall appearance of hanging baskets. Woolly and glaucous (bluish-grey sheen) leaf surfaces can prove very attractive in the right setting, and finely dissected, filigree foliage can often add a new dimension to your basket planting.

Ten types to try

Spider plant (*Chlorophytum comosum*)

Usually treated as a houseplant, the variegated form of the spider plant (*C. comosum* 'Variegatum') is ideal for outdoor summer baskets.

Display: striking cream-banded leaves; sends out arching stems (stolons) that bear a combination of small white flowers and plantlets. Ideal as central focal feature in baskets.

Site: In sun or deep shade.

Propagation: Detach small plantlets from stems in spring or summer, and peg these down into pans or small pots of compost to encourage rooting.

Flame nettle
(*Solenostemon*)

Previously listed under *Coleus*, selected spreading forms make eye-catching basket plants. Named basket varieties to look for include: 'Blackheart' — very dark leaves with green margins; 'Lord Falmouth' — crimson, brown and green margins; and 'Rob Roy' — cerise centre, surrounded by a black halo, and green scalloped margins.

Display: Incredible varied range of leaf form and coloration. Superb as solo plants, or as vigorous fillers in larger baskets.

Site: Sheltered site shaded from direct hot midday sun.

Propagation: Increase good forms by rooting soft cuttings in spring or summer. Seeds of mixtures such as 'Fashion Parade' grow about 9-12 in (23-30 cm), and should be germinated in warmth during early spring.

Ground ivy
(*Glechoma*)

The white-variegated form of our native ground ivy (*G. hederacea* 'Variegata') is perfectly hardy, and widely offered. One of the most common components in mail-order basket collections, but sometimes affected by disfiguring powdery mildew disease in hot, dry weather.

Display: Long trails of slender stems bearing small leaves liberally splashed with bold white markings. Plant at top or sides.

Site: Grow in sun or light shade. The long, trailing growth is shown to advantage in baskets hung at high level.

Propagation: Cuttings taken in spring.

*An attractive display of flame nettle (*Solenostemon*) makes the perfect foliage filler for this hanging basket.*

Helichrysum

Two shrubby species are commonly offered, *H. petiolare* and H. *microphyllum*. The former is liable to swamp neighbouring plants in small baskets unless the woolly shoots are periodically pinched back.

Several forms are available. 'Aureum' ('Limelight') has yellowish foliage, while 'Variegatum' has creamy-coloured leaf markings. More compact forms include 'Roundabout', with silver and gold variegations, and the dwarfer, compact 'Goring Silver'. *H. microphyllum* has a

*Surfinia petunias interplanted with blue fan flower (*Scaevola*) plus foliage subjects* Cineraria maritima *and* Helichrysum petiolare.

more restrained, spreading habit and is a better choice for smaller baskets. The leaves are small and silvery.

Display: Trailing habit. The silver-leaved types are wonderful when used as a contrast to very intense flower colours, and all are excellent as a complementary foil to pastel or light shades in colour co-ordinated plantings.

Site: Full sun is essential to prevent straggly growth. Plant at side or top of baskets.

Propagation: Increase by taking cuttings in spring or early autumn and overwinter young plants in frost-free conditions.

Lotus

Desirable for its trails of silver or grey foliage, *Lotus* is also noteworthy for the display of brilliantly coloured, claw-like flowers during spring and summer.

Display: *L. berthelotii* has long trails of silver filigree foliage, with the bonus of orange-red flowers, while *L. × maculatus* is a free flowering hybrid with grey foliage plus red and yellow blooms.

Site: This group are sun-lovers, and look best when planted to trail down the sides of baskets.

Propagation: Take cuttings in spring or early autumn.

Lysimachia

Several species offer the choice of yellow-leaved and variegated forms that make very useful foliage plants. Neither of the species mentioned should ever be allowed to dry out, and both will need copious watering when grown in full sun.

Display: Half-hardy *L. congestifolia* (syn. *L. lyssii*) is a good all-round basket subject, with clusters of maroon-centred, yellow flowers set against a backcloth of dense, semi-trailing growth. The variety 'Goldilocks' provides the bonus of yellow leaf colour, and there's also a gold and green variegated version offered as 'Outback Sunset'.

The perfectly hardy perennial *L. nummularia* also has an elegant golden-leaved form, 'Aurea', and this always looks its best during the summer flowering period.

Site: *L congestifolia* is a superb solo plant for sheltered hanging baskets and wall containers of all kinds. Alternatively, incorpor-

Lysimachia nummularia *'Aurea' in a half basket*

ate it into mixed plantings at the sides, or as a filler. The long, trailing stems of *L. nummularia* 'Aurea' are ideal for the sides of mixed plantings, and look particularly effective when combined with orange-red or blue flowers. Partial shade or sun.

Propagation: Take basal shoot cuttings, or divide overwintered plants in spring.

Oxalis

Several *Oxalis* species have coloured foliage, but the bulbous *O. tetraphylla* 'Iron Cross' has particularly attractive, large, three-lobed foliage that's distinctly marked in the manner suggested by its name.

Display: 'Iron Cross' is a near-hardy form. Its clover-shaped leaves have dark blotches on each leaflet and it produces a crop of long-lasting pink flowers during June and July. *O. triangularis* is a similar, slightly hardier sort: its large reddish-purple leaflets are broadly banded with purple along the margins of the upper surface.

Site: These plants prefer a sunny situation, but they will tolerate a little shade. Use as top fillers.

Propagation: Division of bulb clusters in spring.

Candle plant (*Plectranthus*)

The variegated forms of candle plant are best known as houseplants, but in recent years they have proved excellent, easy foliage subjects for outdoor hanging containers. Two separate types are offered: *P. forsteri* 'Marginatus' (*P. coleoides* 'Marginatus'), and *P. madagascariensis* 'Variegated Mintleaf' (*P. coleoides* 'Variegata').

Display: Vigorous arching growths make a superb foil for

flowering plants, each stem bearing leaves similar to those of the flame nettle and up to 2½ in (6.5 cm) long. 'Marginatus' has irregular, creamy-white leaf margins, while the distinctive (and pleasant) smell produced by the foliage of 'Variegated Mintleaf' gives extra interest.

Site: Ideal for sunny or partially shaded positions. Makes a useful top central focal plant.

Stonecrop (*Sedum*)

Several stonecrops can be incorporated into basket planting schemes, but one of the most useful is the variegated form of the tender *S. lineare*. This half-hardy perennial succulent is quick-growing and moderately drought-resistant. Offered by larger, well-stocked garden centres and specialist succulent nurseries.

Display: Trailing *S. lineare* 'Variegatum' has eye-catching foliage and is ideal for combining with fairly restrained flowering plants in small or medium-sized baskets. The foliage is needle-like and striped with white. Other useful stonecrops include the hardy *S. sieboldii* 'Mediovariegatum'; its clustered, flattened, grey-green leaves have a central band of yellow.

Site: Stonecrops prefer a sunny site and are useful for side and top rim planting positions.

Propagation: Take stem cuttings in spring or summer.

Nasturtium (*Tropaeolum*)

Besides their glorious flowers, certain varieties of *T. majus* have very decorative foliage. One of the most attractive varieties is 'Alaska', a compact, non-trailing modern hybrid with

Stonecrop (Sedum morganianum)

light-green leaves sprinkled and splashed in creamy-white. Garden centres sometimes offer plants of 'Alaska'; all are available as seeds.

Display: 'Alaska' grows up to about 9 in (23 cm) tall, and plants produce flowers that are held well clear of the foliage — colours include dark-red, orange, pink and yellow. Also look out for the trailing variety 'Jewel of Africa', which has variegated leaves.

Site: Nasturtiums love sun. Use compact types as top fillers, and trailing types on the sides.

Propagation: Sow seeds in late winter or early spring.

Shady characters

The range of flowering plants that can be relied on to give a bright show in shade is somewhat limited. However, many of the plants mentioned in previous sections will tolerate some shade. Even so, you shouldn't expect first-class displays if they're planted in baskets that languish in a permanent state of deep gloom!

But gloom doesn't have to lead to despondency. Several of our favourite summer bedding subjects are quite at home in shadier corners of the garden.

The majority of those listed here are superb subjects for solo plantings, and can be used to create spectacular, blocks of dense colour where it's needed most — in those difficult, dreary areas of shade cast by trees, buildings, and high fences.

To these resilient flowering plants you can add a selection of shade-tolerant foliage subjects. Some of these are mentioned in other parts of the book, but for convenience they've been listed again in the panel at the end of this section.

Begonia
Begonia hybrids
Modern hybrids derived from the fibrous-rooted *B. semperflorens* abound. This popular summer bedding plant is very versatile, and most varieties will succeed just as readily in shade as in sunshine. Depending on variety, you can choose white, red or pink flowers, and foliage colour can range from deepest green to chocolate-brown and bronze.

Solo plantings can look attractive, but adding at least one variety of foliage plant will often enhance the effect even more.

Tuberous-rooted *B. sutherlandii* has only recently been recognised as one of the most useful species for baskets in shade. From quite small tubers, the plants grow at a phenomenal rate: in ideal growing conditions one plant will fill up an average-sized basket in a single season. It produces arching stems liberally clothed with small, pale-green leaves, and constantly covered by a succession of small, dainty, orange flowers.

Plants of *B. semperflorens* are usually discarded at the end of each display season, but the tubers of *B. sutherlandii* can be stored in a frost-free place during the winter period, then started into growth in warmth each spring.

Begonia semperflorens *makes a superb solo plant for hanging baskets in shady or full sun situations.*

Trailing bellflower
Campanula isophylla

This delicate beauty comes in blue- or white-flowered forms, and provides a succession of flowers over a long period. Although ideal for shady situations, it will also give a grand show in well-lit spots.

The trailing bellflower is available as a plant, or can be raised from seeds sown in winter for flowering in the same year. 'Kristal' is a modern seed strain giving relatively large flowers in white or blue, and occasionally gives rise to individuals with grey, woolly foliage. This bellflower may also be increased by means of cuttings rooted in autumn or spring.

Try this perennial as a solo subject in small baskets, or set it in the side of a basket carrying a mixed collection of plants. 'Kristal' and other forms are hardy in many areas of Britain, but good specimens are best overwintered in a greenhouse or conservatory.

Campanula isophylla

Fuchsia 'Marinka'

Fuchsia
Fuchsia hybrids

Although fuchsias were mentioned as summer-flowering
shrubs, they fall just as easily
into this category.

A few varieties derived from
naturally pendant species can be
left to their own devices after
one stopping. They includes the
well-known single-flowered
'Marinka' (scarlet sepals and
corolla), single 'President
Margaret Slater' (white sepals
and mauve-pink corolla),
double-flowered 'Swingtime'
(red sepals and white corolla),
and single 'Temptation' (pink-
flushed, white sepals and
bright, reddish-orange corolla).

Other basket varieties should
be pinched out on a more
regular basis, or there's a ten-
dency for plants to develop long
lengths of flowerless shoots,
with colour concentrated at the
tips. In practice this will result
in baskets with a ring of flowers
hanging around the sides, but
poor coverage on the top.

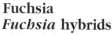

*Prolific busy lizzies are equally at
home in sun or shade.*

Busy lizzie
Impatiens hybrids

This easily grown half-hardy
perennial is one of the mainstays of summer colour. It's one
of the most versatile of garden
plants, and despite its tropical
origins the popular busy lizzie
provides an unbroken succession of flowers from late spring
until the first frosts.

The choice of varieties grows
year by year, ranging from
ground-hugging dwarfs to
vigorous, large-flowered New
Guinea hybrids displaying
beautifully decorative foliage. F1
hybrids abound. They include
low-growing 'Accent' in a range
of red, pink and white shades,
and bicoloured selections with
white-starred red flowers. Fl
'Swirl' is a recent stunner which
produces an abundance of
blush-white blooms with a
distinctive pink picotee petal
edging.

Shady partners

Maidenhair fern (*Adiantum*): Ideal species for partial shade or deep gloom include *A. capillus-veneris* and *A. raddianum*.

Chlorophytum: Both the plain green-leaved species, *C comosum*, and the white-striped form 'Variegatum' succeed in deep shade.

Ivy *(Hedera)*: Many forms of our native ivy, *H. helix*, make wonderful displays in deep shade. Spreading variegated sorts like 'Glacier', 'Sagittifolia Variegata', 'Little Diamond' and 'Midas Touch' are ideal for baskets.

Tradescantia: Many forms of this popular trailing houseplant are ideal for outdoor display in summer. Ideal types to use include *T. fluminensis* varieties such as white-striped 'Quicksilver' and 'Maiden's Blush', with pink, green and white leaves, and *T. zebrina* with silver, green and purple foliage.

Periwinkle (*Vinca*): Variegated forms of evergreen hardy species make ideal trailing partners for shade-loving flowers. These include *V. major* 'Variegata', *V. minor* 'Argenteovariegata' and *V. minor* 'Aureovariegata'.

Top: Chlorophytum comosum 'Vittatum'

Bottom: Adiantum capillus-veneris

Double and semi-double varieties are also on the increase, and pale-pink, rose, red and white are joined by the occasional bicolour. Fl hybrids such as 'Confection Mixed' and 'Rosette' are in this category, both forming rather low, bushy plants that are ideal for top positions in baskets.

Busy lizzies look particularly stunning when used as solo plants in all types of hanging container, but they are also very useful for providing mass colour effect in mixed baskets. One special method of displaying this beautiful bedder is to plant up a 'flower ball' comprising two baskets wired firmly together — grown well, the effect is unbelievable!

During the spring you'll find a wide range of busy lizzie plants in garden centres and stores, but if you have a greenhouse or conservatory you can reduce costs by ordering plug or pot-ready plants from mail-order suppliers and growing these on to maturity. Seeds of most varieties are readily available, but they need constant high temperatures to encourage germination.

Monkey musk/Monkey flower
Mimulus

These moisture-loving perennials are best sited in a sheltered, semi-shaded spot. A whole range of fine Fl hybrids is available, and these provide plenty of scope for colour, with

Prolific Begonia semperflorens *makes a welcoming display at the front door.*

flowers in cream, yellow, orange, and red, some delicately spotted or boldly blotched in contrasting colours.

Vigorous hybrids such as Fl 'Calypso', 'Sparkles', and 'Malibu' can be grown as solo plants, or in association with other shade-loving foliage or flowering subjects. Plants grow from 6 to 9 in (15 to 23 cm) tall and can be used for sides and tops of baskets.

As a rule plants are readily available at garden centres, or you raise them from seeds sown under glass in late winter or early spring. These prolific

perennials need large amounts of water in summer, and as they tend to flower themselves to the point of exhaustion, they are best discarded at the end of each season.

67

Culinary fillers

Fruit and vegetables don't immediately spring to mind as basket fillers, yet there's no reason to preclude them for their lack of flower power. Vigour will be the restraining factor, so your choice is necessarily limited to a few varieties noted for their naturally restricted growth habit.

If you want to create a culinary feature that will please the eye as much as the palate, adding some colourful versions of culinary herbs will help to brighten things up. Most herbs have highly aromatic foliage, and this will be more noticeable as the weather warms up.

The fruits of tomatoes and strawberries will provide some welcome colour as they come into cropping. You can even, without cheating, add some carefully chosen ornamental flowering plants — several have edible leaves and flowers!

Almost all the plants listed below prefer a sunny situation, but there are several exceptions, and I've noted tolerance to shade where applicable.

Given the restricted amount of rooting space, you must be careful to keep fruit and vegetable varieties well supplied with moisture, and to give

A hardy selection of variegated herbs including purple sage and variegated thyme.

growth and cropping a boost with judicious feeding. Soft-growing herbs such as mint will also benefit from similar treatment, but perennial woody herbs like thyme will not relish overfeeding, and may well respond by losing much of their scent and flavour.

Vigorous growers like sage and many mint varieties can be used to great effect, but you'll usually need to pinch them back periodically to stop them overwhelming less rampant neighbours. This will give you material for the kitchen, and any shoot tips left over need not be discarded: they can be dried or frozen for future use.

Named varieties of many perennial herbs are available only as young plants. Common forms are usually offered by larger garden centres, but you may need to consult specialist catalogues for less well-known sorts. Common culinary herbs are readily raised from seeds sown in spring. Sow hardy annual herbs in April, and half-hardy sorts in March. Germinate the latter under glass, and move them outdoors in May.

If you want to maintain named varieties for the following year, most can be overwintered in a sheltered part of the garden. If their hardiness is suspect, move them into a cold greenhouse or frame. Hardy herbaceous types such as mint can be propagated by dividing the rootstocks in early to mid-spring, and shrubby sorts by rooting cuttings in summer.

Vegetables and fruit

Cucumber
Cucumis sativus
'Bush Champion' is the most suitable outdoor variety for planting in hanging baskets. It has a compact growing habit and produces plenty of tasty fruits, each reaching 8–9 in (20–23 cm) in length.

Sow seeds singly in small pots, and germinate them in a heated propagator or warm room in late April. After hardening the young plants off, plant outdoors in early June. Male and female flowers should both be left on the plants.

Cucumbers prefer a warm, sheltered spot in full sun or partial shade.

*Bowle's mint (*Mentha rotundifolia *'Variegata')*

Tomato
Lycopersicon esculentum
Outdoor dwarf bush tomato varieties are the most likely to succeed in the restricted growing space of a basket. Of these, the Fl hybrid 'Tumbler' is probably the best variety to grow. It displays a cascading habit that doesn't need stopping or training, and it's a prolific cropper, producing masses of cherry tomatoes. An alternative is Fl hybrid 'Tornado', an early heavy cropper providing good-sized fruits with an excellent flavour.

Young plants are offered by some larger garden centres, and seed is widely available. Germinate seeds in a heated propagator in early spring.

Set one tomato plant in each 14 in (35 cm) basket. You can have contrasting colour by adding a few ornamentals, such as blue or white lobelia, around the sides. A constant water supply and regular feeding are

Top: *'Cambridge Favourite' is an attractive miniature strawberry.*

Below: Basil (Ocimum basilicum) *'Dark Opal'*

essential to maintain healthy plants and continuous cropping until the first frosts.

Tomatoes prefer a warm, sheltered spot in sun or partial shade.

Strawberries
Fragaria × ananassa

Strawberries are the only group of fruit that can be grown in baskets with any likelihood of success. Look out for perpetual or everbearer varieties like 'Aromel' or 'Calypso'. Once established, these will begin cropping in late June, and continue producing through the summer and into the autumn.

As choice of varieties is likely to be rather limited at garden centres, you may have to obtain young plants from mail-order specialist fruit growers. The varieties recommended above are also listed in some major seed catalogues.

Alpine strawberries (Fraise de Bois), recognisable by their bushy habit and lack of runners, produce small fruits — but they have prolific cropping potential, and the flavour of the fruit is superb. Larger garden centres occasionally offer plants, and seeds of several varieties are widely available.

As the Alpine varieties are derived from a wild woodland species, they prefer partially

shaded conditions. Varieties include 'Baron Solemacher'; 'Alexandria', which bears relatively large fruits for this group; and 'Mignonette', a variety that bears slightly larger fruits than 'Alexandria', used in France to decorate cakes and pastries.

The Alpine types have given rise to a new group of strawberries which produce larger fruit without losing the distinct aroma and flavour. 'Mara des Bois' is typical: it combines the vigorous growth of the perpetu-

al type with the flavour of the woodland species. This one is offered as a young plant through mail-order outlets.

Two recent introductions are Fl hybrids 'Sweet Sensation' and 'Temptation'. These compact, runner-free varieties should be sown in January or February and germinated in a warm propagator to give plants that begin to crop in mid-July or August. Seeds are offered by most of the major seed houses, and plug plants are occasionally offered by mail order.

Herbs

Basil
Ocimum basilicum
This half-hardy annual comes in a number of different forms and varieties. You can buy plants from garden centres or stores, or sow seeds under cover in March or April and set young plants in position in late May or June. Unlike many other herbs, basil loses much of its flavour when dried, and is best frozen in ice cubes.

The plain green sweet basil is very useful, but perhaps not as decorative as others. 'Green Bouquet' is a compact, dome-shaped selection clothed in small but strongly flavoured leaves. A frilly-leaved form is also available. It grows to 10-12 in (25-30 cm). Add leaves to green salads, or use to flavour egg, fish, meat and tomato dishes.

Red or purple basil is very decorative, but just as tasty as the green. Frilly-leaved 'Purple Ruffles' is especially effective for a decorative herb basket, and makes a good contrast with its green counterpart. It adds colour and taste to salads, and it's ideal for flavouring pasta and tomato dishes.

Chives
Allium schoenoprasum
A perennial member of the onion family that produces tufts of grass-like leaves with a distinctive mild flavour. Remove flower buds to encourage succession of fresh leaves.

However, if two specimens are planted, you can allow one to produce the delightful globular heads of lavender-pink flowers in summer.

Chives grow up to 12 in (30 cm) tall. Chop the leaves finely and add to potato salad, stuffed eggs, soups, sauces and salads. Cut leaves down to within 1 in (2.5 cm) of the compost when collecting for use. Leaves can be cut from March until October.

Plants are widely available. Propagate by division or sow seeds in March.

Marjoram
Origanum
A whole range of varieties is available, some of which bear decorative foliage. Sweet marjoram (*O. majorana*) is the one commonly used in the kitchen It grows about 12 in (30 cm) tall, and is treated as a half-hardy annual. For colour, try hardy perennial golden marjoram or oregano (*O. vulgare* 'Aureum');

it grows 6 in (15 cm) tall, with yellow foliage and pink flowers. Pot marjoram (*O. onites*) is another hardy perennial reaching 15 in (38 cm) in height and bearing purple-pink flowers.

Sprinkle chopped leaves on meat before roasting, use as a final garnish on soups, and add to salads. Leaves of all types can be collected and dried or frozen for winter use.

Plants of hardy perennial types are also available. Sow seeds of half-hardy sweet marjoram under glass in early spring. Propagate hardy types by division in spring.

Chives (Allium schoenoprasum)

Nasturtium
Tropaeolum majus
Although not strictly a herb, the leaves of the common nasturtium are perfectly edible. In the case of the compact-growing variety 'Alaska' the leaves are sprinkled and splashed with cream and white, making them even more decorative, yet no less palatable.

Add the peppery-flavoured leaves to salads. The flowers are also edible, and make an unusual addition to salads, as well as a providing a welcome splash of colour among the rather muted hues of herbs.

Plants of 'Alaska' are occasionally available at garden centres. Alternatively sow seeds in early spring.

Parsley
Petroselinum crispum
The curly-leaved varieties of parsley are most suitable for hanging baskets, since they only grow about 12 in (30 cm) tall and have attractive, dense, frilly foliage.

Parsley is one of the finest garnishes available, and is used with thyme for stuffing poultry. It's an ingredient of bouquet garni, and superb when finely chopped and added to white sauce served with fish. Leaves may be frozen or dried.

Container-grown plants are widely available in late spring and summer. Alternatively sow seeds in April for summer cropping. Plants will usually overwinter to give early cuttings the following year.

Parsley grown for use as well as ornament in a highly attractive hanging basket display.

Mint
Mentha
Most mint varieties are rather large for planting in hanging baskets, but one or two that don't achieve such rampant growth can be used in large containers. However, two decorative varieties that seem to behave in a more restrained fashion when restricted to baskets are the pineapple mint, *M. suaveolens* 'Variegata', and the curly-leaved version of common mint, *M. spicata* 'Crispa'.

Pineapple mint has attractive cream-and-green variegated foliage — add to vegetables, salads and fruit salads. Use curly mint with vegetables and salads.

Plants are widely available from larger garden centres, and by mail order from herb specialists. Propagate by taking cuttings of soft, unflowered shoots in mid-spring and early summer. Alternatively divide roots in early spring.

Sage
Salvia officinalis

This hardy semi-evergreen shrub is available in a number of decorative varieties. *Salvia officinalis* 'Icterina' has gold-and-green variegated foliage, but tends to be rather spreading. 'Purpurascens' has purple leaves, but the compact growing 'Tricolor' is possibly the best for hanging baskets. This one has grey-green leaves splashed and flushed with creamy-white, pink and purple.

Sage is a very strongly flavoured herb that should be used in moderation. It's an essential ingredient for stuffings in conjunction with poultry, pork and veal.

Plant young plants, and either prune back hard the following spring or replace annually. Propagate new plants of colour varieties by taking cuttings of half-ripe shoots, when the lower part of the stem is just firm, from early to mid-summer.

Thyme
Thymus vulgaris

Growing only 6 in (15 cm) tall, the bushy common thyme is suitable for even the smallest hanging basket. However, two coloured-leaved variants will provide decoration as well as culinary service. *Aureus* is a slightly taller thyme with yellow-tinted foliage, while 'Silver Posie' has fine white-and-green variegated foliage. All are highly aromatic.

Thyme, one of the most popular herbs, is used alone for rubbing on meat prior to roasting, and is an ingredient for poultry and other stuffings. Use sparingly on fish dishes, and add to soups and stews.

The hardy common thyme is widely available, and both decorative varieties are usually offered by larger garden centres and specialist mail-order suppliers. Seeds of common thyme are readily available, and should be sown in early spring. Decorative types are increased by means of softwood cuttings rooted in early summer.

Ornamental herb Salvia officinalis *'Tricolor', a colourful form of the common culinary sage.*

Evergreen fillers

There's a surprisingly large number of dwarf and moderate-sized evergreens that are suitable for planting in hanging containers. Almost all are shrubby, but several of the smaller hardy evergreen ferns can make an attractive contribution to autumn, winter and spring displays.

You might raise your eyebrows at some of the more vigorous shrubs I'm going to suggest, but here the secret is to use young plants and replace them before they can overwhelm their neighbours. The Japanese laurel (*Aucuba*) is typical of this group. Luckily it's easy to propagate from autumn-rooted cuttings, which should ensure a steady succession of replacements!

Use evergreens to form the backbone of winter and spring basket displays. Generally speaking their flowers have little, if any, significant role, but they do have the important job of creating a permanent foil for the more flowery components of each planting scheme. They also help to provide height and a focal point in each planting arrangement.

As long as your compost remains well drained and fertile, most of these plants can be left *in situ* for a number of years. Only the seasonal bedding plants, such as pansies, have to be replaced every year. How-ever, the more vigorous types will need repotting as the top growth and root systems become congested. As a rule, you'll need to carry out a major overhaul every two or three years.

All the following evergreens are offered as plants, and most are widely available from any well-stocked garden centre. You can supplement this list with several hardy evergreen plants already mentioned as summer foliage fillers (see the section on foliage fillers).

Aucuba japonica '*Variegata*'

Ten easy evergreens

Japanese laurel
Aucuba japonica

A hardy shrub that can eventually grow 7–10 ft (2–3 m) tall, but may be used as a top focal plant for a maximum of two years in larger basket arrangements. Good for shady positions, but best results in the open come from two variegated forms that are fairly easily found: 'Variegata', with glossy, yellow-speckled leaves, and 'Crotonifolia' ('Crotonoides') featuring large, golden-spotted and blotched foliage.

Euonymus

Vigorous and very hardy evergreen available in a wide range of attractive variegated varieties. Ideal for baskets positioned in sun or shade, it can easily cope with exposed situations. Depending on the size of the basket, plant at the top and sides.

For smaller baskets the slow-growing, *E. japonicus* 'Microphyllus' is ideal, since the leaves are small and the habit dense and compact, giving it an almost box-like appearance. Varieties to look for include 'Microphyllus Pulchellus', with leaves suffused with yellow, and white-margined 'Albovariegatus'. Both grow up to about 12 in (30 cm) tall and as much across.

E. fortunei has larger leaves, and a wider, more vigorous, spreading habit. This means it

Euonymus fortunei *'Emerald Gaiety'* *and 'Emerald 'n' Gold'*

can't be used in baskets for more than a couple of years, at the most. Look for the variety 'Emerald 'n' Gold', with deep-green leaves bearing a broad yellow margin in summer, later turning cream and flushed pink in colder weather. 'Emerald Gaiety' has irregular white leaf margins, which also take on a pink tinge in winter.

Cuttings of short side-shoots root readily at almost any time in a cold frame or greenhouse.

Ferns

A number of hardy evergreen ferns make attractive additions to hanging basket displays. All are ideal for situations ranging from light to deep shade.

Forms of the hart's tongue fern, *Asplenium scolopendrium* (syn. *Phyllitis scolopendrium)*, are particularly attractive and useful for top planting positions. 'Kay's Lacerated' is a dwarf form with deeply cut fronds growing 9–12 in (23–30 cm) long, while 'Cristatum' grows a little taller, with fronds that are topped by a finely cut crest or tassel. 'Muricatum' is another, growing 9–18 in (23–45 cm) tall with narrow, crinkly fronds.

The leathery, medium-green fronds of *Cyrtomium falcatum* make an excellent central focal point in a winter basket, and at 1–2 ft (30–60 cm) will fit comfortably in all but the smallest hanging container.

Other less well-known types to look out for include *Dryopteris erythrosora prolifera*, which produces bronze-tinged new fronds that are finely divided and grow no more 12 in (30 cm) tall, and *Polystichum tsusimense*, an excellent, neat fern growing up to about 9–15 in (23–38 cm) tall with short, dark-green fronds.

Hebe

In the main, only the small-leaved, heather-like hebes are hardy enough and small enough for use in winter hanging baskets. Of these, 'Emerald Green' ('Green Globe') is probably the best choice, since it forms a compact, bun-shaped bush up to about 12 in (30 cm) tall. This little gem has a dense arrangement of glossy green leaves and small, white blossoms that appear in summer.

In milder regions, the attractive cream-edged leaves of *H. × franciscana* 'Variegata' make it a superb top centre focal plant, but away from coastal areas it needs a sunny site sheltered from cold winds.

Widely available as a pot plant, this variety makes a dome-shaped plant and bears dense clusters of blue flowers in summer. Both types of hebe can be readily increased by rooting cuttings under glass during spring and summer.

Ivy
Hedera

The ivies make superb all-year display plants. Varieties noted for their useful trailing habit and hardiness include: 'Irish Lace', with green, narrowly lobed foliage; silver-variegated 'Ceridwen' and 'Little Diamond'; and golden-variegated 'Goldchild'.

All are readily available as pot plants, and easy to propagate by means of cuttings rooted in mid to late summer. Ivies are ideal for shady spots; plant them at the sides or tops of containers.

Hedera helix 'Glacier'

Curry plant
Helichrysum italiacum

This ornate herb has limited culinary uses, but it's very desirable for its year-round display of decorative foliage. Evergrey rather than evergreen, *Helichrysum italicum* (syn. *H. angustifolium*) grows 2 ft (60 cm) or so tall. Each erect stem is clothed in silver-grey needle-like leaves and topped by a cluster of bright-yellow flowers in summer.

The dwarf and compact *H. italicum microphyllum* is one of the best sorts for hanging baskets, as it only reaches l2in (30 cm) in height and has very silvery foliage.

The curry plant has a very distinct curry-like aroma, and needs good light to produce stocky, well-coloured growth. Plants are widely available and ideal for top planting positions. It makes an excellent centre plant for winter basket display in a sunny spot. Increase by means of summer-rooted cuttings.

Honeysuckle
Lonicera

The small-leaved, densely growing *L. nitida* is the only species suitable for hanging baskets, and then only for a season or so. 'Baggesen's Gold' is particularly attractive: the new leaves are yellow in summer, gradually turning yellow-green as the colder weather sets in.

This non-climbing honeysuckle can be kept within bounds by clipping, and is suitable for medium to large baskets in sun or shade. Plant in a top position.

'Baggesen's Gold' is widely available as small or medium-sized container plants. Propagate by rooting short lengths of fully-ripened shoots (hardwood cuttings) in a cold frame or greenhouse during late autumn or early winter.

Variegated forms of Helichrysum petiolare *make ideal complementary companions for flowers in pastel shades.*

Osmanthus

O. heterophyllus is a slow-growing evergreen shrub that is often mistaken for holly. Although it eventually grows quite large, young specimens of selected forms and varieties can make attractive additions to hanging baskets on a short term basis.

'Goshiki' is an unusual variety, producing bronze-tinged young foliage that gradually takes on a conspicuous yellow mottling. Other varieties that could be tried include 'Variegatus', with cream-bordered foliage, and yellow-margined 'Aureo-marginatus'.

Plant in centre top position and site in sun or partial shade. 'Goshiki' is fairly widely available, otherwise consult specialist mail-order shrub catalogues. Propagate with semi-ripe shoot cuttings rooted in a heated propagator from early to mid-autumn.

Lavender cotton
Santolina

These neat little evergreens form dense, low mounds of green, grey or silver foliage. In summer these are topped by numerous button-like yellow or cream flowers. *S. rosmarinifolia* has bright-green, thread-like foliage and lemon-coloured flowers, while its variety 'Primrose Gem' has pale-yellow flowers. Both grow up to about 12 in (30 cm) tall.

S. chamaecyparissus has silvery-white felted foliage and lemon-yellow flowers; the variety 'Nana' is a denser, more compact selection growing about 12 in (30 cm) high, while 'Small Ness', at only 9 in (23 cm) tall and 12 in (30 cm) across, is ideal for smaller baskets.

A sunny site is essential for *Santolina*, otherwise growth becomes drawn and straggly. Plant it in top or side positions. Both species are widely available, but look for dwarf selections of *S. chamaecyparissus* in shrub catalogues. Increase by rooting semi-ripe cuttings put into a garden frame between early and mid-autumn. Alternatively take hardwood cuttings in late autumn or early winter.

Thyme
Thymus

I've already mentioned several culinary thymes (at the very end of the chapter on summer displays), but there are many other hardy evergreen species and forms that can be used as winter or year-round fillers.

Low-growing *T. citriodorus* (lemon-scented thyme) is available in a range of delightful aromatic selections, some of which have both culinary and decorative uses. 'Archer's Gold' forms mounds of yellow and green foliage 3–4 in (7.5–10 cm) tall, while silver-variegated 'Variegatus' makes bushy plants 6 in (15 cm) tall and about the same in width.

Two other low-growing, spreading thymes to look out for are 'Doone Valley' and *T. serpyllum* 'Goldstream', both golden-variegated beauties that bear pinky-mauve flowers in summer.

Thyme is best in full sun, and can be planted in the sides or tops of baskets. Increase plants by dividing low-growing species in spring, or by rooting cuttings of shrubby sorts in early summer.

White-painted walls are in stark contrast to colourful containers. This timber wall basket is amply clothed with hardy trailing creeping jenny and a selection of half-hardy summer bedders.

Bedders and bulbs

Once you've made your choice of evergreens, the next stage is to add some bright colour to the winter and spring display. Traditional spring bedders such as pansies and primroses continue to provide the bulk of colour for hanging baskets, but in recent years a growing number of perennial herbaceous ground-cover subjects have been recognised as valuable companion plants. Their ornate foliage and flowers can provide welcome additional interest.

Hardiness is the keyword for successful winter basket displays. Ideally you should try to ensure that greenhouse-raised spring bedding plants are well established in their final outdoor positions before the onset of

hard weather. In practice, this means that winter and spring baskets should normally be planted up some time between mid-September and mid-October.

Plant breeders have made great strides in producing better and brighter spring bedding plants. You can see the results in the excellent current range of Fl hybrid pansy, primrose and polyanthus varieties. Cabbages, too, can provide Fl hybrid colour: the Japanese-bred ornamental kales will give months of unexpected interest, though you won't want to cut them for the pot!

Arabis caucasica *'Variegata'*

Cold weather colour

Bugle
Ajuga

Low-growing *A. reptans* is a creeping herbaceous perennial plant that retains some foliage during the colder months. This moisture-loving subject is happy in sun or shade, and suitable for side or top-edge planting positions in baskets.

The foliage forms are most widely grown, and most produce attractive spikes of blue flowers from late spring into summer. 'Atropurpurea', the purple bugle, has eye-catching bronzy-purple leaves; 'Multicolor' ('Tricolor' or 'Rainbow'), the salamander bugle, has yellow and reddish checked foliage, while 'Variegata' has cream-and-pink variegated leaves.

Young plants are available by mail order, and as container-grown stock from garden centres. Propagate by dividing the crowns in autumn or spring, or by pegging down runners to root during spring or summer.

Rock cress
Arabis

Also commonly called wall cress, *Arabis* includes a number of very hardy trailing perennials that need good drainage and plenty of sun.

A. ferdinandi-coburgii and its forms are useful for side plantings or for trailing over the rims of baskets. This species only grows about 3 in (7.5 cm) tall, and produces numerous white flowers in spring. Two good

white, pink and red shades, and they grow up to about 6 in (15 cm) tall. Varieties to look out for include 'Pomponette' and 'Spring Star'.

The button daisies are offered as mail-order plants, or you can get them from larger garden centres and stores. Seeds are also available, and you should sow them in late spring or early summer for planting out in autumn. Plant them in top edge positions. These daisies are suitable for sun and shade.

selections to try are 'Old Gold', with yellow leaf variegation, and silvery-white splashed 'Variegata'.

A. caucasica is more vigorous, reaching up to about 6 in (15 cm) tall. Interesting forms to look for include 'Plena', with double white flowers, and 'Variegata', featuring silver-and-gold leaf variegations.

Container-grown plants are available throughout the year. Increase rock cress by dividing the plants in October, or rooting cuttings in summer.

Daisy
Bellis

The small, double-flowered button varieties of *B. perennis* are suitable for hanging basket displays in spring and early summer. You can buy the modern versions in a range of

Alpine heath
Erica carnea

Winter-flowering *E. carnea* could fit just as well in the preceding section, but I've included it here because its long flowering season can be very useful. Many fine cultivars are

*Daisy (*Bellis) 'Pomponette Red'*

widely available from specialist suppliers, and these provide a succession of colour from November through to April. Most flower from late winter into early spring.

'Springwood White' is widely available from garden centres. Its rather trailing shoots are packed with white blooms during winter and early spring. 'Springwood Pink' is another mid-season sort, while 'Vivellii' has superb, deep-carmine flowers held above foliage that turns bronzy-red at the onset of cold weather.

Unlike other heaths, *E. carnea* will tolerate some lime in the soil, which makes it suitable for mixed winter basket plantings.

These sun-loving evergreens grow about 6–9 in (15–23 cm) tall, and make excellent subjects for top planting positions in baskets.

Deadnettle
Lamium

Now firmly established as a first-class basket plant, this creeping ground-cover perennial is used in much the same fashion as bugle. *L. maculatum* provides the largest number of forms, with decorative foliage and pink or white flower trusses in late spring and early summer. Growth tends to decline somewhat with the onset of winter, but regenerates rapidly in spring.

The following selections are widely offered by garden centres, and often appear in mail-order basket collections:

'White Nancy' features leaves that are wholly silver, and white flowers; 'Beacon Silver' has silver foliage with a narrow green margin and purple-lilac flowers; while 'Aureum' is a rather compact slow-growing type with yellow leaves, each bearing central white stripes.

The yellow archangel, variously known as *Lamium galeobdolon, Lamiastrum galeob-*

Top: Erica carnea *'Foxhollow'*

Above: Lamium maculatum *'Silver Beacon'*

dolon, and *Galeobdolon luteum,* is a vigorous creeping plant that has yielded several desirable forms. The evergreen types are most useful for winter display. They include 'Florentinum', with bright-green, nettle-like leaves that are speckled silver and take on a reddish tinge in winter; 'Silver Carpet', with green-veined silver foliage; and the similarly marked 'Hermann's Pride'. All have bright yellow flowers.

Semi-trailing deadnettle is suitable for side or top positions in sun or partial shade, while yellow Archangel prefers partial or full shade. Both grow up to around 8 in (20 cm) tall.

*Forget-me-not (*Myosotis*) 'Victoria Rose'*

Creeping Jenny
Lysimachia nummularia
The golden-leaved form of creeping Jenny (*L. n.* 'Aurea') makes an ideal spring foliage subject for hanging baskets in a partially shaded site. It produces a succession of yellow, chalice-shaped flowers throughout the summer, which helps to prolong the display from winter baskets.

Keep creeping Jenny well supplied with moisture in spring and summer, with more moderate watering during the cooler months. Plant this creeping herbaceous perennial in side and top rim positions. Plants are widely available from garden centres and by mail order. Increase plants by dividing clumps in autumn or spring.

Forget-me-not
Myosotis
This is a traditional bedding plant for spring displays, invaluable for its profusion of blue, pink or white blooms on plants growing up to 12 in (30 cm) tall. Though technically a perennial, *M. sylvatica* is usually treated as a hardy biennial: sow seeds in early summer for flowering the following year. Mail-order plug plants are available from some major seed companies.

Many cultivars are available from seeds, including 'Royal Blue', growing up to 12 in (30 cm) tall, 'Carmine King' at 8 in (20 cm), or 'Victoria Mixed', which produces uniform plants in shades of white, rose and pink. 'Magnum Blue' grows up

(Above): Myosotis *'Victoria Rose'*

(Below): Pansies *(*Viola × wittrockiana*)*

to 6 in (15 cm) tall; it's very prolific and is sometimes offered as plug plants. *Myosotis* prefers sunny situations, and provides welcome colour in top planting positions.

Ornamental kale
Brassica oleracea
hybrids

This colourful relative of the cabbage has become a popular plant for winter container displays. Single plants look good in medium-sized or large baskets, and established, potted individuals are now widely available in larger garden centres and stores. You can buy young plants by mail order.

A selection of attractive Fl hybrids is now available. These give you the basic foliage colour you'd expect from a cabbage, but with a central leaf rosette in shades of rose, pink and white. The most popular is 'Northern Lights', which can measure 18 in (45 cm) across and grows 9 in (23 cm) tall. Other sorts include 'Osaka', and 'Peacock', a very attractive mixture with finely cut, filigreed leaves.

Seeds are sown under cover in spring for planting out in autumn. Suitable for sunny and partially shaded situations.

Primrose and polyanthus
Primula

These winter and spring stalwarts provide welcome colour during the cold weather. This group is now available in a wonderful range of vivid colours, with several strains featuring attractive bronze-red foliage. Primroses produce numerous short stalks bearing single flowers, while polyanthus sends up stout stems about 6 in (15 cm) tall, each topped with a cluster of blooms.

If you start Fl hybrid plants early they'll begin giving colour in early autumn, with further sporadic flushes of flowers in mild periods during the winter. However, you'll enjoy the main display in spring.

Mail-order seedlings and pot-ready plants are available during late summer and early autumn, and established, well-budded plants are offered by all garden centres and stores.

The following range of Fl hybrid primrose and polyanthus cultivars is available as seeds and frequently as plants:

'Husky' is a lovely compact primrose mixture giving red, pink, white, yellow and blue flowers peeping out from rosettes of bronze-green foliage. 'Paloma' has dense, richly coloured clusters of primrose blooms. Polyanthus 'Crescendo' displays large bright flowers in a wide range of colours, while 'Rainbow' is an extra-hardy mixture providing a superb range of colours.

Primroses and polyanthus are happy in a sunny or partially shaded situation. Plant them in top basket positions. Start seeds in spring or early summer to give strong plants for early autumn planting, or propagate by dividing the rootstocks just after flowering has finished.

Summer pansies (Viola × wittrockiana)

Pansy
Viola × wittrockiana

This easy and attractive bedding plant provides most of the colour in hanging baskets during the drab months of the year. It was originally grown as a hardy biennial for spring and summer display, but new Fl hybrid forms have been developed to give almost year-round interest.

The group widely known as winter pansies are the most valuable for earliest displays. These perform in much the same way as primroses and polyanthus, giving flushes of flowers at any time the weather is mild. Selections that have proved most reliable in bad weather include the 'Universal' series, and especially the recent 'Universal Plus' which gives a very good range of colours.

This series includes a good mix of clear-coloured selections, along with others that have a distinctive dark 'whiskering' or blotching. You can also obtain seeds in at least ten single-colour selections. Fl 'Ultima' is another superb mixture containing an excellent range of colours. Both grow up to around 6 in (15 cm) tall.

I've already mentioned the smaller-flowered 'Princess' series in the summer-flowering section, but you can also plant it for winter and spring displays.

Pansies are equally at home in sun or partial shade, and suitable for side or top basket planting positions. Sow seeds in summer.

Early bulb colour

Windflower (*Anemone*)

This is a large group, but the easy and prolific *A. blanda* provides welcome basket colour in late winter and early spring. The normal flower colour is shades of blue, but there are a number of excellent selections such as 'White Splendour', 'Violet Star', the deep-pink 'Charmer', and the white-centred, red 'Radar'.

Plant the rounded rhizomes 3 in (7.5 cm) deep in October or November. A small basket will take about ten rhizomes in a top planting position.

Anemone blanda *'Pink Star'*

Crocus tommasinianus

Crocus

A wonderful, prolific group that provides colour from late January into spring. Earliest to bloom are the species crocuses like *C. chrysanthus* and *C. tommasinianus*, both growing about 3 in (7.5 cm) tall. Cultivars include 'Cream Beauty' (*C. chrysanthus*), yellow 'E. P. Bowles' (*C. chrysanthus*), white 'Snow Bunting' (*C. chrysanthus*), ruby-violet 'Ruby Giant' (*C. tommasinianus*) and 'Whitewell Purple' (*C. tommasinianus*).

The larger-flowered Dutch hybrids are also suitable for hanging basket display; these flower slightly later than the species sorts and are frequently offered in mixtures. For individual colours try white 'Jeanne d' Arc', 'Pickwick' with violet feathering over a grey-white ground, and 'Golden Yellow', which may also be variously named 'Mammoth', 'Yellow Giant' or 'Dutch Yellow'. All grow about 5 in (13 cm) tall.

Plant corms 3 in (7.5 cm) in the autumn. Put them in the sun, in a side or top position. Crocus are ideal in mixed winter collections, and the larger Dutch sorts also make eye-catching features when planted on their own.

Grape hyacinth (*Muscari*)

Grape hyacinths are prolific bulbs that give an extended display of blue or white flower spikes throughout the spring. *M. armeniacum* sends up dense spikes of vivid blue flowers up to 6 in (15 cm) tall, while *M. botryoides* 'Album' has pure white, fragrant flowers.

The blue grape hyacinth is excellent as a solo plant in small baskets, but you can use all types in top or side positions in mixed plant collections. Plant bulbs 2–3 in (5–7.5 cm) deep in autumn. Grape hyacinth prefers a sunny situation.

Daffodil (Narcissus) *'Hawera'*

Muscari botryoides *'Album'*

Daffodil (*Narcissus*)

Only the short-stemmed daffodils are suitable for baskets, but there are numerous hybrids that are very useful companions to complement pansies, polyanthus and primroses in spring. Types to try include: 'Hawera', a dwarf Triandrus narcissus growing up to 8 in (20 cm) tall and bearing several small, lemon-yellow, slightly fragrant flowers; the Cyclamineus hybrid 'Jack Snipe', featuring single yellow trumpet flowers with reflexed white petals; and the all-yellow Jonquil hybrid 'Baby Moon', a scented multi-headed beauty with small blooms at the top of 8 in (20 cm) tall stems.

Plant bulbs 3–4 in (7.5–10 cm) deep in autumn. Put them in a top position in sun or partial shade.

Tulip (*Tulipa*)

The dwarf-growing early flowering tulips are ideal for medium or large basket sizes. One of the finest is the double-flowered 'Peach Blossom', with dense, globular heads of deep pink flowers topping 10 in (25 cm) stems in April. Other types to try include 'Red Riding Hood', a *greigii* tulip with red flowers on 6 in (15 cm) stems and beautifully mottled foliage, and *kaufmanniana* tulip 'Johann Strauss', a white-and-yellow beauty that flowers in March.

Plant bulbs 4 in (10 cm) deep in top positions. Tulips need a sunny site to produce their best colour.

Baskets in the home

Just browse around any garden centre with a well-stocked houseplant section and you'll be amazed at the range of plants suitable for indoor high-level display. Many of the hardy and half-hardy perennial plants suggested in other sections of this book are equally effective, if not better, when grown under cover, but the tally rises in step with an increase in temperature.

Several of the plants listed here will tolerate frost-free conditions, but I advise main- taining a minimum winter temperature of at least 40-45°F (4-7°C) to keep most of them in good condition.

Tropical and sub-tropical plants needing slightly warmer conditions will benefit if you can maintain a minimum winter temperature of 50-55°F (10-13°C). You may find it too expensive to keep a conservato- ry at this temperature: if so, there's a simple solution. Just move your favourite plants into the home until weather condi- tions improve.

In the main, it's best to devote indoor hanging containers to a single plant type, but there's no hard and fast rule that says mixed plantings can't be done. However, my advice is to limit combinations to two plant types: one major feature plant, and a less vigorous companion to spill over the edge of the container.

*Wandering Jew (*Tradescantia blossfeldiana*) and emerald fern (*Asparagus densiflorus*) are both easy foliage subjects for high-level display.*

Baskets for cool conditions

Emerald fern
Asparagus densiflorus 'Sprengeri'
Also known as *A. sprengeri*, this isn't really a fern at all — but it is extremely useful for its prolific arching stems, which are covered in bright-green, needle-like leaves. It grows well in partial shade or well-lit spots out of direct sunlight. Increase by division at any time of the year.

Bush violet
Browallia speciosa
Several types are offered from seed or plants, but modern sorts like the blue or white-flowered 'Troll' series are ideal for basket work.

Buy them in flower, sow them in spring for summer display, or sow them in summer for winter colour. They're suitable for a bright position out of direct summer sun.

Variegated Italian bellflower
Campanula isophylla 'Mayi'
This easy plant likes good light, but not direct summer sun. It produces trailing stems clothed with variegated felt-covered leaves.

The plants become a mass of blue-mauve saucer-shaped flowers in summer. Root stem cuttings in spring.

(Above): Asparagus densiflorus

(Below): Browalla speciosa *'Blue Bells'*

Kalanchoe manginii

A superb spring-flowered succulent producing a profusion of clustered, pendant, bell-shaped flowers in a range of pink, orange and coral shades. Hybrids such as 'Wendy' and 'Tessa' are widely available from larger garden centres. Increase by rooting stem cuttings during spring or summer. Hang in a well lit location.

Cape cowslip
Lachenalia bulbifera

You'll need to order bulbs of this unusual South African plant from specialist bulb suppliers in spring for planting up in August. Plant six bulbs in each 5 in (12 cm) hanging pot, or space out 1–2 in (2.5–5 cm) apart in open mesh baskets — push a few through the sides to give better cover. The loose clusters of purplish-red or pink flowers are produced in spring. Repot bulbs annually, and increase with bulblets at potting time.

Greenhouse orchid
Coelogyne cristata

This is one of the easiest orchids for beginners. It's ideal for timber-slatted or open-mesh baskets filled with special orchid compost (available from mail-order specialists).

Grow in partial shade in summer. In late winter or spring, well-grown plants will bear a profusion of white flowers marked with orange-yellow. Propagate by dividing clumps of pseudobulbs after flowering.

A Columnea *hybrid in tandem with the Fiji fern,* Davallia fejeensis.

Fiji fern
Davallia fejeensis

Wonderful fern with glossy, carrot-like fronds that sprout from strange, hairy, creeping rhizomes. Widely offered by garden centres, and particularly attractive when grown in hanging terracotta pots. Increase by pegging down sections of rhizomes in compost, or divide in spring.

Mother-of-thousands
Saxifraga stolonifera

This is a superb, near-hardy foliage species that sends out numerous runners up to 2–3 ft (60–90 cm) long, each tipped with a miniature replica of the mother plant. Ideal for hanging pots in good light or shade. Masses of delicate pink-marked white flowers may be produced in spring. The smaller, slow-growing variety 'Tricolor' has attractive leaves that are red on the lower surface and white

Kalanchoe manginii

variegated on the upper surface. Increase by pegging down runner tips in summer.

Burro's tail
Sedum morganianum
A superb succulent plant that produces long, trailing stems densely clothed with grey-green leaves. Perfect drainage and good light are essential for this very easy, attractive plant. Well-grown specimens may produce cascading shoots over 2 ft (60 cm) long.

Trailing violet
Viola hederacea
A novel, near-hardy Australian species that spreads by means of runners. This charming plant bears numerous purple or white violet flowers during the summer months. It's ideal for small hanging pots in partial shade. Increase by pegging down runners in spring or summer.

(Below, left): Lachenalia

(Below, right): Saxifraga stolonifera (sarmentosa)

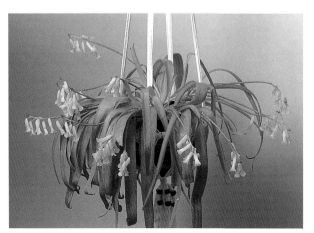

Plants for warm settings

Hot-water plant
Achimenes

This summer-flowering exotic is grown from tiny tubers (tubercles) planted in late winter or early spring. Many beautiful hybrids are available as tubers

Achimenes *'Rumpelstiltskin'*

from mail-order catalogues, or you can buy flowering plants from garden centres. The plant produces masses of vibrant red, pink, purple and violet flowers over dark, rather coarse foliage. It needs good light, but shade it from direct summer sun. It hates cold draughts. Gradually decrease watering as the flowers fade, and store tubers in a cool place until the following year.

Lipstick vines
Aeschynanthus

This colourful group of exotics needs warm, humid conditions to encourage a display of clustered, yellow-marked, red, orange or purple tubular flowers throughout the summer. Lipstick vines send out arching stems clothed in rather succulent, waxy leaves. Look out for species such as *A. speciosus* and hybrids such as 'Little Tiger'. Protect from direct summer sun, and mist frequently, especially in summer. Increase by rooting soft shoot-tip cuttings in spring.

Columnea

These are close relatives of the lipstick vines, but produce hooded flowers in shades of glowing yellow, red and orange. *C.* × *banksii* is one of the easiest types, but *C. gloriosa* (goldfish plant) has even more attractive trailing stems that will totally obscure the container. Also look out for variegated types such as *C. microphylla* 'Variegata' and *C. hirta* 'Variegata' (syn. *C.* 'Light Prince'), along with modern hybrids like 'Stavanger' and 'Merkur'. Treat in the same way as lipstick vines (*Aeschynanthus*, above).

Creeping fig
Ficus pumila

A dense, creeping plant that makes a superb specimen for free-hanging or wall-mounted containers. The ordinary green-leaved plant is easy, but the variegated form is more attractive. Put this in a shady spot — direct sun is lethal! Keep compost uniformly moist at all times, and mist over leaves frequently.

Above: Columnea tricolor *in a hanging basket*

Below: Ficus pumila *(variegated form)*

93

Nephrolepis exaltata

Miniature wax plant
Hoya bella

A superb little plant that produces arching growths tipped with clusters of small, fragrant, pale-pink flowers any time between late spring and early autumn.

Avoid planting it in large containers, and hang it in a shady spot. Mist regularly when the plant is out of bloom, and water carefully from autumn to spring. Increase by rooting tips of shoots in spring.

Polka dot plant
Hypoestes phyllostachya

Also called 'freckle face', this attractive plant has beautifully marked leaves which are liberally splashed with silver or silvery-pink spots.

Many selections are now available, but site them in good light or the foliage may lose its colour. Remove flower buds as they appear, and regularly prune back erect shoots to keep them about 12 in (30 cm) tall. Sow seeds in spring or propagate by taking stem cuttings in spring and summer.

Sword fern
Nephrolepis exaltata

This erect-growing, tender fern has several very desirable forms with graceful, arching fronds. The Boston fern, *N. e.* 'Bostoniensis', is widely available from garden centres and stores, and this one is ideal for locations that allow good, indirect light. Mist over fronds regularly to maintain humidity. Propagate by dividing the rootstock in spring, or by pegging down the delicate runners that grow out from the plant.

African violet
Saintpaulia

Several attractive, trailing versions of this popular houseplant are currently offered by larger garden centres and specialist mail-order suppliers. Single and double-flowered varieties are available, and a range of miniature sorts make superb small-scale hanging features. Give them a well lit position, but shade them from direct, hot summer sun. Occasionally mist over the plants when they are out of flower, but don't let water remain on the crowns. Leaf cuttings root at almost any time of the year.

Cape primrose
Streptocarpus saxorum

Unlike the popular hybrid florist varieties, this species sends out sprawling stems clothed with fairly small, succulent leaves. The small trumpet flowers are pale-blue with a cream throat, and they're borne in profusion from mid-summer to autumn. Modern hybrids also make excellent subjects for hanging containers indoors, but ensure they are given good light and plenty of moisture in the growing season. Increase by division or leaf cuttings in spring or summer.

Wandering Jew
Tradescantia fluminensis

One of the easiest trailing houseplants, and one that lends itself readily to high-level display, *T. fluminensis* comes in a range of white and pink variegated foliage forms, including 'Albovittata' and the beautifully striped 'Quicksilver' — but I must make special mention of the fairly recent pink, purple and white-leaved introduction called 'Maiden's Blush', which changes colour according to the temperature. The related *T. zebrina* is another popular species, and here again a range of silver, pink and purple-flushed forms is available. All prefer good light, and cuttings should be taken regularly to provide replacements as old plants become straggly.

Tradescantia fluminensis
'Quicksilver'

Index